What Investors are Saying abou

I was paying enormous fees for my 401k and the
no longer pay thousands every year just to have so ...j money.
I only wish I'd have known about the eQRP® a decade earlier.

Tom Burns, MD
Syndicator, Author, Speaker

In this book, Damion does a masterful job explaining in simple terms exactly what an eQRP® is, how it works, and why it's arguably one of most powerful structures a Main Street investor has available to take back control of their financial future.

Of course, savvy investors can (and should) use the knowledge in this book to help their prospective investors unlock the power of big chunks of their balance sheets.

They say knowledge is power ... when acted upon.

In this case, the knowledge to tap into $40 trillion of potential investment capital is in the pages ahead when YOU discover the power of the eQRP® and incorporate them into your successful syndication business.

So read, learn, and take effective action ... to grow your investment business helping people take back total control of their retirement plans with the eQRP®.

Robert Helms and Russell Gray
Hosts
The Real Estate Guys™ Radio Show

The Secret Retirement Plan for MD's to get Full Control of their 401k & IRA money!

Eric Tait, MD, MBA
Founder, The Physicians Road Podcast

I was blown away when I learned about the eQRP, and now I rave about it to all of my Real Estate Goddesses! And all my goddesses who have been referred are thrilled.

Monick Halm
RE Investor Goddesses Founder.

After vetting Damion and talking to many financial planners whom were respected in their fields I took the plunge and set up MY eQRP® and was scared to death. I was terrified about having all this power at my fingertips (or in reality checkbook) and how I could invest in almost anything tax free.

Then, I took a deep breath, and wrote a check that is currently yielding a way higher return on my retirement $ than I'd ever get in the stock market and I didn't have to ask any custodian for permission (think Self Directed IRA). I can make unlimited investments with my eQRP® incurring zero transactional fees cutting out the middleman. The options are limitless and with Damion's help I can now have total freedom over my wealth building strategies while getting all the benefits of gains growing tax free or tax deferred.

Mark Podolsky
Founder, Land Geek

Converting traditional IRAs to eQRP®s has been a game changer for Wealth Formula Investors, saving us millions of dollars in unnecessary taxes!

Buck Joffrey, MD
Founder, Wealthformula.com

I came to the eQRP® because I wanted to get away from Wall Street and direct my own retirement. I continue to say how great my experience has been and am amazed at how available the eQRP® team is at any time. I've been so moved by my experience I'm thrilled to referred my friends to eQRP®.

Patricia Cooper

I've always followed the advice of advisors. I allowed my advisor to take control of my investments and the market's been really good to me. However, my good friend has developed a real estate syndication deal that seems really interesting and I want to get involved with.

My eQRP® gave me the flexibility and opportunity to invest in this deal and potentially make gains greater than expected and I get to be in control and experiment for myself.

Yanmin Tao

Since joining the eQRP® I have learned more about how money works and the different ways to leverage this. The eQRP® creates a great environment of knowledge and education to help you make better/informed decisions while having an expert always ready to help you when you need it. They really do an excellent job on coaching you, no matter what level of investor you may be!

Elisa Norton

We were able to roll over $120,000 from my previous employer's 401k into my own eQRP® after I left the company. I was then able to convert all $120,000 to Roth in the first year because my wife is a Real Estate professional which allowed us to offset the taxes induced by the Roth conversion with our passive depreciation from real estate investments. This saved us more than $40,000.00 in income taxes. Thanks eQRP®!

Thero Mitchell

I was able to roll the full amount of my Thrift Savings Plan over into my eQRP® after I retired from the Army.

This gave me the control of my money from the limited index funds in the TSP and purchase multiple syndications that have already begun cash-flowing at a greater rate of return than the average annual growth of my TSP over the previous 20 years.

I'm also able to purchase precious metals to hedge my portfolio and legally hold those Gold Eagles in my own safe, giving me the ability to personally protect and maintain the gold.

Mark

I'm so grateful we learned about the eQRP®! We thought self-directed IRAs were the best way to invest, having check-book control of the money. But once it came time to sell the property our SDIRA owned, we were gonna be hit hard with UDFI taxes due to debt on the property. The eQRP® Co. solved our problem and avoided the UBIT tax by converting the IRA over to an eQRP®!

It literally took a 15-minute phone call to get things rolling, now that's what I call simple. And you are accessible by phone call and email for all our questions going forward. Thanks for all your help.

Isaac & Mara De Los Reyes

I'm a real estate investor and I'm also a member of biggerpockets.com. One of my friends from the bigger pockets community introduced me to the self-directed IRA and checkbook control 401(k) about three years ago. I didn't have a self-employed side hustle at that time, so I set up a SDIRA and invested in a few real estate syndications. I was pretty happy with what I did until later on when I realized that I would be hit by 37% Unrelated Business Income Tax (UBIT) when my syndications conduct a sale since they are 65% leveraged.

I knew I had to move my investment to a self-directed solo 401(k) to avoid the UBIT. With many options out there, I did my research in terms of cost, ease of rollover, reputation, knowledge, and support.

Eventually I settled with eQRP® since it's a well-known company and a well-known product within the real estate community. I also read their books about eQRP® and had a few phone calls before making the decision. **It's not the cheapest, but just like anything in life, you get what you pay for. I want the product and services to be the best in the space.** So I believe that eQRP® is the right fit for my needs.

Bishan Colon

My wife Krista and I are happy customers. We have already invested in two private equity deals so far and are looking forward to more, it was "checkbook easy." Now I just need to generate more self-employment activity income and we will be off to the races.

Daniel Markert

My sister fell on hard times last year and I was able to loan her $40K from my eQRP®. It's good to be the bank!

I listened to Damion's interview with John Casmon and his message completely resonated with me. The fact that I reached financial freedom in a mere 2.5 years of investment in real estate is a great example of why it makes sense for people to take control of their own financial future instead of letting Wall Street take control of their money and charge exorbitant fees from mediocre management jobs.

So in the end, I think self-education, control of one's money, and trying things out beat ceding control of one's own money to Wall Street. No matter how you look at it.

Jun Wang

"For years, the lack of control I had over my OWN MONEY in my 401k was a serious source of frustration for me. I've always viewed the stock market as a form of gambling, so I didn't want to send my money to Wall Street – and I don't like bonds or treasury notes, because of out-of-control government spending. So that left only 1 choice inside my 401k… Cash. As a result, years went by with my entire 401k being 100% stuck in cash, and as the government continued to print more and more cash, my retirement account got less and less valuable, and I got more and more frustrated.

All that changed in 2012. I met Damion Lupo and learned about the eQRP®. After I had my attorney thoroughly scrutinize the plan and give me a double thumbs up approval, I got my own eQRP® set up and took CHECK-BOOK CONTROL of my own money. Now my retirement money is 100% MINE to invest the way I want.

If you're anything like me, you absolutely owe it to yourself to get an eQRP®!"

Jon Butcher,
Founder LIFEBOOK

"Damion's team have been exceptional in putting together and helping me get my eQRP® set up! I have comfort in knowing that I have control over my money and best of all I don't have to deal with cumbersome paperwork every single year!"

Dr. Angelica Farrell,
Chiropractor / Business Owner, Salud Chiropractic

QRP Book

How to get all the money you need for your deals.

Plus, how to invest your 401k or IRA in things like:

- ✓ *Real Estate*
- ✓ *Gold & Silver*
- ✓ *Bitcoin*
- ✓ *Almost anything*

DAMION S. LUPO, CCIM

QRP Book

Copyright © 2022 by Damion Lupo

Inquiries should be addressed to:

eQRP Media
30 N Gould St Ste R
Sheridan WY 82801

www.QRPBook.com

First Edition

First Printing August 8th, 2013

Cover design by Casey Dahnert

ISBN	Softcover	978-1-945057-12-0
	Hardcover	978-1-945057-11-3
	Kindle	978-1-945057-13-7

1. Retirement Plans 2. Financial

AUTHOR'S NOTE

This book is designed to provide general information pertaining to the subjects discussed including retirement accounts. Laws and general practices vary from state to state and change constantly. With each situation different, specific advice for specific situations should be obtained by the reader's own advisors pertaining to the reader's situation.

The author has taken reasonable precautions in preparing this book and believes the facts are accurate as of the date it was written. Many of the thoughts, ideas and opinions are subjective and relevant to the current environment. They could change based any number of evolving environments, laws and geopolitical shifts. Neither the author nor publisher assumes any responsibility for any errors or omissions. The author and publisher specifically disclaim any liability resulting from the use or application of the information contained in this book, and the information is not intended to serve as legal advice related to individual situations.

The author highly recommends you consult with your advisors, including your attorney and accountant about any plans you may have or are considering and that you get their professional opinion and advice before taking any action.

FOREWORD

Eric S. Tait M.D., MBA
The Physician's Road – Where You Create
Your Life in Medicine on Your Own Terms

Have you ever known about someone before you actually met them? That was my experience with Damion Lupo. We ran in the same circles and attended the same conferences, yet I could never quite figure out how his business helped investors.

Damion was often surrounded by a group of people, all very engaged in discussion with him. Watching this repeatedly, I knew he had something special to offer.

It wasn't until many of our own investors began lamenting the fact that they couldn't easily access their tax-deferred retirement account money to invest in our projects that I realized how powerful Damion's approach was.

So, I sat down with him at an investment conference and really dug into his business, and the power of the account he offers to his clients.

Imagine – you're a busy physician in private practice. You're maxing out your tax-deferred accounts every year. You realize that 90% or more of your investment portfolio value is in the publicly traded stock and bond market.

Or maybe you're an employed physician with an old 401K/IRA from a previous employer. You're in the same position -90% of your investable assets are in the volatile publicly traded markets.

What can you do?

The problem with most "retirement" plans is that you're stuck with the basic menu of options your custodian gives you.

The usual investment professionals' mantra is "diversification at all costs." But can you truly be diversified if the bulk of your investment net worth is in the same pool of publicly traded assets?

During the financial crisis of 2008-2009, all publicly traded asset classes went down in price, which theoretically should not have happened in a "diversified" portfolio.

If you only have stocks and bonds, then by definition you're not diversified. You have no private market exposure.

The eQRP can help change all that.

Now you can control your money while still maintaining tax deferred status.

You may be asking yourself, "Why haven't I heard of this type of account before?"

The honest answer is there just isn't much money to be made in administering this type of account. Typical Wall Street/Financial Services firms have no incentive to promote this money saving account because if they did, they wouldn't be able to charge you on your money or gain a commission by purchasing mutual funds for you.

They say new ideas take a long time for acceptance, and the eQRP is no exception. Without the backing and marketing machine of Wall Street behind him, Damion is waging a guerilla marketing campaign to give investors back control of their money and their sense of power.

As physicians, I think this resonates with us. Our autonomy is constantly under assault in the medical profession, and it feels as though everyone takes advantage of us. It can leave us feeling powerless.

That's why I love the eQRP account - it allows us to take back control of our hard-earned dollars and makes us the captain of our own ship.

No more middlemen and women taking account fees without adding value to our investment process. Just gentle guidance from Damion's team to make sure that we use our newfound power wisely and within the bounds of acceptable practice.

But with great power comes great responsibility. You have to be ready to take ownership over your financial future.

This doesn't have to be hard or complicated. In fact, we think simple is best. And now you have the tool to actually invest in things that you understand.

No more Wall Street doublespeak if you don't want it.

You can create a truly diversified portfolio by being able to invest in not only publicly traded stocks and bonds but also privately held real estate and private businesses.

All this while keeping your tax-deferred status.

This book is your gateway to a different financial future, one where you can chart your own course- independent of financial planners and fees if you so choose.

The eQRP is about freedom - the freedom to stay the course or the freedom to change it, without having to "ask permission."

You can even open a ROTH within your account as you see fit.

The eQRP is truly the most powerful retirement account on the market, and I'm glad Damion and his team offer it. It could revolutionize your investment strategy.

Contents

SECTION I - The Dirty Details
(To go to the Quick Overview, go to section 2)

SECTION 5

SECTION 6

SECTION 7

INTRODUCTION

If you're a Syndicator or you want to put deals together with other people's money this may be the most important book you read this year.

If you have money in a retirement account and feel uncomfortable stuck in the Wall Street Casino, this book is your ticket to exiting that roller coaster and moving to total control of your financial future.

As of 2022 investors in the United States held retirement account assets in excess of $40,000,000,000,000, that's 40 trillion dollars.

Most of that money is stuck in Wall Street paper assets they can't control and are getting charged to death with fees by the institutions to handle the assets while the return to the investor is basically crap.

Whether you're creating deals for other investors or investing in those deals, the power of the eQRP is putting the power of money back in the hands of the people. This tool allows the investor to take control of their money inside a checkbook where you get to sign the checks doing deals you choose!

Imagine every time you put a deal together and call a list of 10 people you know who had previously built up 401ks and IRA's – that they now have checkbook control of their money. Your next million or 10 could simply be a few phone calls away.

In this book you will learn how to use this tool and how to share it with people you know, love and care about so you can all create wealth together and you'll never again wonder how to fund your next deal, or feel your money is stuck on Wall Street.

Please contact me on LinkedIn if I can ever be of any help to you or answer any questions about the eQRP or anything else. Always happy to hear from self-responsible people like you who are willing to invest time and money into books like this.

I am deeply honored you chose to invest your time with me and I'm here to help you succeed.

To Freedom,
Damion S. Lupo, CCIM

"Everything popular is wrong."

- Oscar Wilde

Wall Street Propaganda: The Spring 2012 issue of Charles Schwab's investing newsletter includes an article on 401ks and states:

The key piece of information the author leaves out is that when you have anQRP, which is a type of self directed 401k you have way more flexibility, control and protection that any form or version of an IRA. But they wouldn't want you to know that. We do.

> "The age-old idea of putting money into the stock markets and getting an 8-10% fixed reliable return without being savvy, i.e., "passive dumb income" is a dead idea. Those days are over."

- Bill Gross, PIMCO

The purpose of this book is to provide individuals with a Rollover 401k from their previous employer with the knowledge and understanding of retirement plan options available to them. Not only will this book provide you with the opportunity to learn about the many tax advantages of having a Checkbook Control Plan, but it also describes the features of qualified plans that can reduce both the cost and complexity of implementing and maintaining one.

LEARNING OBJECTIVES

After reading this book you will be able to:

- ❏ Compare the advantages and disadvantages of qualified and non-qualified retirement plans.
- ❏ Analyze the tax and non tax benefits of a qualified retirement plan.
- ❏ List the basic steps in establishing a qualified retirement plan.
- ❏ Contrast features of the various types of 401k plans.
- ❏ Describe the basic requirements of maintaining a qualified retirement plan.

INTRODUCTION

Today, the American dream is to have the ability to set aside funds to plan for retirement and unforeseen financial emergencies. However, in today's ever changing economy, finding the extra money to save for the future may seem impossible for many workers. This is especially difficult for those employed in small businesses.

Today more than ever, Americans realize the importance of saving for the future. Most experts estimate that the average American will need between $1.2 million to $1.5 million in a retirement plan to provide for a reasonable lifestyle after retirement. They also estimate that 8 months of expenses should be put aside for unexpected financial emergencies or about $30,000 to $50,000 for the average worker.

In order to provide American workers the opportunity to save and plan for retirement, the U.S. Internal Revenue Code provides a variety of tax-advantage retirement plans through which employees may save funds for retirement. In addition, employers can offer retirement plans for employees' that, if they meet certain qualifications under the Tax Code, create tax advantages for both parties.

However, with any qualified retirement savings plan for which the government affords tax breaks, there are requirements, under the current tax code and the *Employee Retirement Income Security Act of 1974 (ERISA)*, for maintaining the plans. For example, plans must be updated to reflect changes in the law and information about the plan must be reported annually to employees as well as the IRS. If a plan falls out of compliance or is inappropriately used for the advantage of the wrong parties, it must be corrected to avoid penalties or the loss of its qualification for special tax treatment.

This section describes the various types of plans which may be appropriate, taking into account the employer's particular resources and objectives. Some qualified plans, called **defined benefit plans**, are structured so that the employee is guaranteed to receive a specific amount of benefits upon retirement and require employers to make contributions.

Defined contribution plans in most cases are more flexible and give employers the choice, rather than the requirement, of contributing to the employee's retirement assets. *(The Safe Harbor plan is has some requirements that are specific to you if you have employees, see The Honey Badger for more information)*. Employers can also offer a 401k cash-deferred arrangement, which permits employees to make elective deferrals of their wages for payment into retirement plans but with the significant tax advantages of a qualified defined contribution plan.

WHAT IS THE EQRP®?

The eQRP is an Enhanced Qualified Retirement Plan. The Internal Revenue Code (Section 401) defines this type of structure as a retirement savings trust. The difference between Qualified and Non-Qualified Plans:

A qualified plan such as the eQRP is a type of retirement savings plan set up by a business that conforms to the requirements of Section 401 of the U.S. Tax code. Since a qualified retirement plan conforms to Section 401 requirements, the plan qualifies for special tax rules that provide small business owners with substantial tax saving opportunities. Some of the most common types of qualified plans are Profit Sharing Plans, 401k plans, and Defined Benefit Plans. One of the biggest advantages is that contributions made by the employer to the plan on behalf of the employee are tax deductible. Contributions are made using pre-tax dollars which allows you to postpone paying income taxes on money contributed giving it time to compound and grow over time. Under ERISA (Employee Retirement Income Security ACT) of 1974, qualified plan investments are protected from creditors, bankruptcy, and the IRS.

The eQRP is the Ferrari of 401k's because of the way all the documents are written and the patented process for giving you liability protection as well as allowing you to hire employees.

Did you know that solo 401k's do NOT have the same ERISA liability protections that big company 401k's have in the event of a lawsuit? That's right, big company plans are bullet proof, solo's are sitting ducks.

Old Solo accounts do not allow the owner to hire anyone. That's right, not even a part time employee let alone full-time employees.

The eQRP allows up to 50 employees part or full time. Everyone gets total control of their money and investment choices!

The eQRP has rock solid protections built in and dynamic flexibility for you to grow your team and wealth making it superior.

It's designed to give you every option allowable by law and is **pre-approved by the IRS** with a letter of preapproval included with your plan. You can truly do anything you want within the framework of what's allowed with the law.

Your eQRP is a highly flexible and tax-efficient retirement solution that allow you to make high contributions to the plan either pre-tax or by designating it a ROTH and making part or all of your assets 100% tax-free for life.

❑ Contribute up to $61,000 a year ($67,500 if you're over 50) *2022 limits
❑ Borrow up to $50,000 or 50% of your account value (whichever is less)
❑ Invest in almost any type of investment tax-free including:

- Real Estate Deals
- Precious metals like Gold, Silver, and Platinum
- Cryptocurrencies like Bitcoin ™
- Tax Liens
- Private businesses
- Private loans
- Stocks, bonds, mutual funds

With an eQRP you're able to use your retirement funds to make almost any type of investment on your own without requiring the "consent" of anyone else like a custodian. The last thing you want is some technical bureaucrat telling you what you can or can't do with your own money, especially when the IRS has been very specific about what the rules are. Why would you limit your choices by working with a custodian? Plus, you must pay fees to this person for the service of telling you no!!!

As a trustee of your eQRP, you will have "Checkbook Control" over the eQRP assets. Unlike a self-directed IRA where you are required by law to have a Custodian who will create pain, friction, delays and endless expenses, with the eQRP you are the one in charge, no outside party telling you what to do and charging you for the pleasure!

The eQRP allows you to invest tax-free in an investment that you know and understand and even allows you to borrow up to $50,000 or 50% of the account for any purpose.

Aside from certain "prohibited transactions" involving Disqualified Persons, which are outlined in the Internal Revenue Code Section 4975, an eQRP can invest in most of the commonly made investments, including real estate, private business entities, public and private shares in companies and commercial and private paper.

Types of Benefit Plans

NON-QUALIFIED PLANS

P lans that do not follow the guidelines and rules Congress has passed into law and thus cannot take advantage of most of the benefits a qualified plan can. (i.e. deferred compensation plans and IRAs)

QUALIFIED PLANS

Qualified retirement plans provide retirement benefits that meet the requirements under federal law. Qualified plans allow employees to defer reporting income from benefits until retirement while at the same time allowing employers to claim a current deduction for contributions to the plans. Income earned by the plan is not taxed to the employees until it is distributed to them as part of their benefits. Almost every type of business entity may establish a retirement plan (sole proprietor, corporation, LLCs and partnerships).

Business owners and their employees can gain significant tax advantages by participating in a company-sponsored retirement plan. Contributions to a qualified retirement plan for yourself and any eligible employees are tax deductible, within tax law limits. All plan participants (including you) can defer paying income taxes until distributions are received from the plan.

Qualified retirement plans provide businesses with a broad range of tax and non-tax benefits. In comparison to non-qualified plans, the qualified retirement plan has more benefits and you can contribute significantly more money. One main requirement of qualified plan is that plan assets must be held in a qualified trust that you can control as the plan administrator. Employers are obligated to offer benefits on a nondiscriminatory basis with respect to salary level to all rank-and-file employees. This requirement ensures that all employees (if any), not just highly paid executives and other key employees, will benefit benefit from the plan.

Additionally, qualified retirement plans are required to contain "anti alienation" provisions that prohibit plan benefits from being assigned or alienated to creditors. This protects your plan assets from creditors and lawsuits. Fortunately, several plan options can make the requirements less burdensome and less costly for small businesses. The combination of tax advantages, variety, and flexibility of plan types makes qualified retirement plans preferable for a majority of small businesses.

WHY HAVEN'T I HEARD OF THE EQRP?

The investment industry has been dominated by 3rd party custodians who have large transaction fees and have limited the investment choices. As trustee of these types of retirement plans, they make money charging transactional and management fees to perform trustee duties.

With an eQRP, you are the trustee and eliminate investment decisions that most likely are not the best for your business and you will also eliminate transactional and management fees that add up over time.

It has also been a misconception over the last 30 years that stocks are the best investments, when in fact a portfolio that is diverse with many types of investments will yield the best return. Your eQRP could be designed to allow you as trustee giving you checkbook control and the authority to invest in alternative investments such as gold and silver, tax liens, business startups, real estate, LLC's, joint ventures, etc.

GENERAL FEATURES OF ALL QUALIFIED RETIREMENT PLANS

Asset Protection

As mentioned previously, assets held in a qualified retirement plan are required to contain "anti alienation" provisions under ERISA. Therefore, pursuant to bankruptcy laws, employer and employee assets in qualified retirement plans are generally protected from creditors including the IRS. I recommend you discuss this with your tax advisor as every situation is different.

Retirement Plans Types

There are two main categories of plans; defined benefit plans and defined contribution plans.

401K PLAN

A 401k plan is a qualified retirement plan that is funded primarily through employee contributions via salary reductions. It was legislatively created in by ERISA in 1974 and by 1981, half of all large corporations had adopted them. Today, use of 401k's is not exclusive to large corporations; even a sole proprietor with no employees can use a 401k. Through a 401k plan, companies have the option to make matching contributions, which vest for participants in the same manner as contributions to other defined contribution plans explained earlier.

Perhaps the most popular type of defined contribution plan today is the 401k plan. The 401k plan allows employee contributions to be made through salary reduction arrangements that let them fund their retirement plan with pretax dollars. These employee contributions are called elective deferrals. Employers often match a percentage of employee elective deferrals as a way to encourage participation, something desirable so that owners, executives, and other highly paid employees can benefit. In addition to pretax contributions, a 401k plan may offer a Roth contribution option.

The Qualified Plans for Self-Employed Individuals

ONE PERSON 401K PLAN

E ven if you work alone, with no employees, you can still have a 401k plan. In 2001 Congress passed EGTRRA which made this possible. This type of plan may enable you to maximize contributions because you can make both employee salary reduction contributions (elective deferrals) and employer contributions.

ROTH 401K

A Roth 401k plan is a separate account through which a participant will make designated after-tax contributions. A Roth 401k plan combines the unique features of the Roth IRA and a traditional 401k plan. The main difference between a Roth 401k and a traditional 401k is that the Roth 401k is funded with after-tax dollars and the traditional 401k plan is funded with pre-tax dollars. While the Roth 401k doesn't get the same upfront tax-deduction as the traditional 401k, the account grows tax-free. Withdrawals taken during retirement are NOT subject to income tax as long as you've had the account for five or more years and are 59 ½ or older.

Key advantages of a Roth 401k:

❑ Annual contribution limits are 10 times higher than in a Roth IRA.
❑ No modified gross income limitations that restrict some individuals from contributing to a Roth IRA.
❑ Participants can keep BOTH pre-tax and after-tax (Roth) savings in a single plan.

A participant may convert their 401k to a Roth 401k commonly called an in-plan rollover. Some guidelines are:

❑ Only eligible rollover distributions may convert; typically rollovers or age 59 ½.
❑ The plan must allow for in-plan Roth conversions and Roth contributions.
❑ Tax paid on amounts converted to Roth (10% tax prior to 59 ½ not applicable)

ROTH 401K ELIGIBILITY

Anyone, regardless of income level, can have a ROTH, as long as the company plan offers it. The eQRP comes standard with a ROTH option. Plan participants can choose to have pre-tax or post- tax (Roth) contributions for their elective deferrals.

Separate accounting is required for the Roth 401k.

ROTH 401K CONTRIBUTIONS

A Roth 401k plan may permit a participant to contribute some or all of their elective deferrals as after-tax contributions. In order to permit after-tax contributions, the plan document must include a choice of both pre-tax and after-tax(Roth) elective deferrals, separate accounts for designated Roth contributions, and must state that only Roth elective deferrals can be contributed to the designated Roth account.

A plan participant has the option to make elective deferrals to the designated Roth account, pre-tax account, or both in whatever increments and proportions they choose as permitted under the plan terms. Total contributions for the Roth account and pre-tax elective deferral cannot exceed the plan annual contribution limit.

One of the biggest advantages of a Roth 401k is that there are no income restrictions. This is very appealing for high-income individuals who haven't been able to contribute to a Roth IRA because of income restrictions. Like a traditional 401k plan, Roth 401k plans are subject to the same contribution limits, which is $20,500 in 2022 and $27,000 for those 50 or older. Roth IRA contributions limits are much less than the Roth 401k ($6000 per year and $7000 if you are 50 or older). Due to the fact that Roth 401k plans are not constrained to the same income restrictions as a Roth IRA, participants can invest thousands of dollars more in tax-free retirement income that the Roth IRA.

Roth 401k contributions are treated the same as pre-tax elective deferrals in the following ways:

- Annual contribution limits
- Mandatory minimum distributions
- Distribution restrictions
- Nondiscrimination testing
- Plan deduction limits (calculation)

Roth 401k contributions are irrevocable, meaning that once contributions are invested into a Roth 401k account, it cannot be moved to a regular 401k account.

A participant cannot make contributions to a Roth 401k for a spouse who has no earned income. A traditional or Roth IRA will allow for a participant to make contributions for your spouse based on their earned income.

Upon termination, a participant may roll the Roth 401k into a Roth IRA.

ROTH 401(K) Distributions

A qualified distribution is not included in your gross income and is generally made after the 5 taxable year period of participation. A distribution is considered a qualified distribution when one of the following criteria are met:

- ❑ The distribution occurs on or after the date you attain age 59 ½.
- ❑ The distribution occurs after your death.
- ❑ The distribution is attributable to you being disabled.
- ❑ You have held the plan for more than 5 years.

It is important to note that distributions that are out of the participant's control, such as plan termination or job termination, are NOT considered qualified distributions (unless you meet one of the qualified distribution criteria listed above). However, in situations like this, you do have the option to do a direct rollover into another designated Roth account.

A non-qualified, in other words, a premature distribution, is subject to the following:

A 10% tax penalty may apply on early withdrawals to the part of the distribution that is included in gross income.

The distribution will be handled as pro-rata from earnings and contributions (basis).

The following distributions are not considered qualified and will include any earnings paid out in gross income:

- ❑ Corrective distribution of elective deferrals in excess of the lesser of $61,000 (2022) or 100% earnings.
- ❑ Deemed distributions from a default on repayment of a loan from the plan.

❑ Corrective distributions of excess deferrals. ($20,500 and $27,000 in 2022 if over age 50).
❑ Corrective distributions of excess contributions.

The 5 taxable year period begins on the first day of your taxable year for which you made the first contribution to the Roth 401k plan. However, if you rollover from a designated Roth account under another plan, the 5 year period begins on the first day of the taxable year that you made designated Roth contributions to the other plan (if this date is earlier than the other).

If you receive a distribution before the 5 taxable year period, it will be considered a non qualified distribution and the earnings must be included in your gross income. Early withdrawals from a Roth 401k are subject to the same rules and requirements as a traditional 401k that we will discuss in the Plan Features section. For the withdrawal to avoid taxation, it must be a qualified distribution and occur at least 5 years from the first Roth 401k contribution or predecessor Roth 401k contribution. Roth 401k contributions will show as deferrals on a W2 and the distributions are reported on Form 1099-R.

A Roth 401k has minimum distribution requirements a participant must begin to receive annually once he/she is the later age of 72 or retires.

ROTH 401(K) Loans

If the plan permits, YES you can take a loan from a Roth 401k. There are guidelines that must be followed in determining the loan amount. A loan from your plan must be combined with all other outstanding loans from the plan and any other plans maintained by the employer.

ROTH 401k In-Plan Rollover

If the plan allows, a participant may transfer eligible rollover distributions to a designated Roth account from another account in the same plan. It is important to note that in order for the plan to accept in-plan rollovers, it MUST be set up to accept elective deferrals from participants. You cannot set up a plan to solely accept in-plan rollovers.

Eligible In-Plan Rollovers

The terms of the plan and other eligible distribution rules will determine the eligible rollover amount. Not all pre-tax balances can be rolled into a Roth 401k plan. An eligible rollover distribution is a distribution that is NOT the following:

- ❏ Hardship distribution
- ❏ Required minimum distribution
- ❏ A loan treated as a distribution
- ❏ A distribution that is one of a series of substantially equal payments made for 10 years or a minimum of once a year over a lifetime.
- ❏ A corrective distribution of excess contributions or deferrals
- ❏ Dividends on employer securities
- ❏ The cost of life insurance

In-Plan Rollover Tax Consequences

An in-plan rollover is not subject to the additional 10% early withdrawal tax. Gains from the in-plan rollover into a designated Roth account are generally subject to a 10% penalty.

The taxable amount of the rollover distribution must be included in the participant's gross income. This is calculated by taking the value of the distribution less the participant's basis. Typically, the entire rollover amount including earnings from a pre-tax account will be taxable. Generally, a plan participant must include any previously untaxed amounts in gross income during the year the rollover occurred.

Once the rollover is complete to a designated Roth 401k plan, it cannot be reversed. The rollover amount cannot be re-characterized or returned to the account it came from.

> *** After you convert a pretax 401k to a Roth 401k you are able to pull the funds out immediately without a 10% penalty because they are considered basis. It does not matter what age you are, this is a secret the rich use to access their retirement accounts early without penalty.

ROTH 401k VS Traditional 401k

When deciding between a Roth 401k and a traditional 401k, many ask themselves, "Do I take a pay cut and invest in a ROTH 401k since contributions are made with after-tax dollars? OR Invest in a traditional 401k and have the tax dollars taken out when I receive distributions at retirement?" If you think you will be in a higher tax bracket at the time of retirement, then it would make sense to invest in a Roth IRA. If you are near retirement age and figure your tax bracket will be lower in retirement, you will benefit from making traditional 401k contributions. Roth 401k plans are desirable to those in high tax brackets who want to pay the taxes now in exchange for the certainty they won't have to pay taxes in the future no matter what tax bracket they are in upon retirement age.

If you still can't decide which plan to invest in, you can invest in both a Roth 401k and a traditional 401k plan in the same year in any proportion you decide.

ROTH

A huge difference between an IRA and the eQRP is for the high earner. Once you reach a certain income level you can not contribute to a Roth IRA or convert a standard IRA to a Roth IRA. You do not have this limitation with the eQRP. You're welcome to contribute up to $20,500 per year into a Roth sub-account of your eQRP, or $27,000 if you're over age 50. You can have both a Roth and regular tax deferral component within the eQRP.

PARTNERSHIP PLANS

An individual partner or partners, although self-employed, may not set up a Self-employed plan. The plan must be established by the partnership. Partnership deductions for contributions to an individual partner's account are reported on the partners Schedule K-1 (Form 1065) and deducted by the partner as an adjustment to income on Form 1040.

> An important distinction between self-employed qualified plans and corporate qualified plans is the way in which contributions are calculated on behalf of owner-employees.

CONTRIBUTIONS TO SELF-EMPLOYED QUALIFIED PLANS

Contributions to all retirement plans are based on compensation. For qualified plans covering employees of corporations, this is simply W-2 taxable wages. For self-employed individuals under self-employed qualified plans, the basis for contributions is a little more complicated. Essentially, the basis for contributions on behalf of owner-employees is net earnings from self-employment. But this is not merely the net profit from your business in which self-employment tax is paid. Net earnings from self-employment must be further reduced by the deduction for one-half of the self-employment tax.

In order to make contributions on your own behalf, you must have net earnings from self-employment derived from your personal services. Almost every activity that you pursue with a goal of making a profit is a business and will qualify you to set up a qualified retirement plan and make tax-deductible contributions. Similar rules apply to members in LLCs.

To calculate compensation of the owner-employee, start with the profit from Schedule C or the net earnings from self-employment on Schedule K-1 of Form 1065. For partners, this is essentially your distributive share of partnership income plus any guaranteed payments. Net earnings from self-employment from various activities are totaled on Schedule SE, Self-Employment Tax. After you have your compensation amount, subtract from this amount one-half of the self-employment tax computed on Schedule SE. This net amount is the figure upon which contributions to qualified retirement plans are based. In order to make contributions on your own behalf, you must have net earnings from self-employment derived from your personal services. If you merely invest capital in a partnership while your personal services are not a material income-producing factor, you cannot make a plan contribution

SET-UP DEADLINES

To deduct contributions for a tax year, your self-employed plan must be adopted by the last day of that year (December 31 if you report on a calendar year basis). If it is, contributions can be made up to the due date of your return for that year, including extensions.

HOW SELF-EMPLOYED PLAN DISTRIBUTIONS ARE TAXED

Distributions from a self-employed plan generally may not be received without penalty before age 59 ½ unless you are disabled or meet the other exceptions. If you own more than 5% of the company, you must begin to receive minimum required distribution by April 1 of the year following the year you reach age 72. If an insufficient distribution is received penalties may apply.

A lump sum and other eligible distributions may be rolled over tax-free to another employer plan or IRA. For participants born before January 2, 1936, 10 year averaging may be available. Pension distributions from a self-employed plan are taxed under the annuity rules, but for the purposes of figuring your cost investment, include only nondeductible voluntary contributions. Deductible contributions made on your behalf are not part of your investment.

Another rule of self-employed plans that is important to note is that after the death of a self-employed plan owner, distributions to beneficiaries may be spread over the periods provided the plan covers more than one person. Distributions to a surviving spouse can be rolled over to that spouse's IRA. The plan may provide that distributions to non-spouse beneficiaries can be rolled over directly to an IRA, enabling them to spread distributions over their life expectancy.

QRP Plan Features

VESTING

While the plan must permit certain employees the opportunity to participate and have contributions made on their behalf, employers have the option to require a certain number of years in the plan before benefits will belong absolutely to the employees. This delay in absolute ownership of benefits is called *vesting*. In order for plans to be qualified, employers cannot defer vesting beyond set limits.

For employer contributions, a plan can provide for *graded vesting*. This permits vesting of 20% of benefits each year after the first year of service. Under this vesting schedule, there is full vesting after six years of participation in the plan.

CONTRIBUTION LIMIT AND DEADLINES

The contribution limit varies based on the type of plan involved. For **defined contribution plans**, the 2022 limit is the lesser of 25% of compensation or $61,000 for 2022. This percentage is the top limit.

For **defined benefit plans**, there is no specific limit on 2022 contributions. Rather, the limit is placed on the benefits that can be provided under the plan. Contributions are then actuarially determined to provide these benefits. For 2022 the plan can not provide benefits exceeding $245,000 per year, adjusted annually for inflation.

Flexibility

Contributions by you to your plan are totally up to you with any type of eQRP. If business is slow and you need to reduce your personal contributions you can slow down or if business is going great you can max out. (If you have employees and have a safe harbor plan you have a minimum required deferral for employees -see the Honey Badger Chapter)

Contribution Deadline

Contributions for defined contribution plans can be made at any time up to the due date of the employer's return, including extensions. In fact, contributions can be made even after the employer's tax return is filed as long as they do not exceed the return's due date. Contributions can be funded through a tax refund.

Example:

An employer (C corporation), whose 2022 return is ordinarily due on March 15, 2022, obtains a filing extension to September 15, 2022. The return is filed on June 1, 2022, and a refund is received on August 15, 2022. The employer has until September 15, 2022 to complete contributions to its profit sharing plan, a deduction for which was reported on the return. The employer can use the refund for this purpose.

The only way to extend the deadline for making contributions is to obtain a valid filing extension. For example, an owner of a professional corporation on a calendar year who wants to extend the time for making contributions must obtain an Extension of Time to file Form 1120. To do this, Form 7004, Application for Automatic Extension of Time to File Corporation Income Tax Return, must be filed no later than March 15, the due date for Form 1120 for calendar-year corporations.

Filing Form 7004 gives the corporation an automatic six-month filing extension, to September 15. The corporation then has until

September 15 to make its contributions to the plan. The type of plan you set up governs both the amount you can deduct and the time when you claim the deduction. Certain plans offer special tax incentives designed to encourage employers to help with employee retirement benefits. Even though you may be an employer, if you are self-employed (a sole proprietor, partner, or LLC member), you are treated as an employee for purposes of participating in these plans.

BORROWING FROM THE PLAN

Within limits, owners may be able to borrow from the plan without adverse tax consequences. The plan must permit loans, limiting them to the lesser of:

- ❑ $50,000 or
- ❑ The greater of one-half your accrued benefit or $10,000

Loans that do not meet the limits above are treated as taxable distributions from the plan. If this occurs, you will receive Form 1099-R.

The loan must be amortized over a period of no more than five years (except for loans that are used to buy personal residences) and charge a reasonable rate of interest. Quarterly payments should be made in substantially equal amounts. You can however make more frequent payments such as monthly payments. It is important to remember that loan repayments are NOT plan contributions.

As an owner, you cannot deduct interest on the loan but the plan pays no tax on the interest income either. The plan must also allow rank-and-file employees the opportunity to borrow from the plan on the same basis as owners and top executives.

LOAN RESTRICTIONS AND LIMITATIONS

- ❑ **Spousal consent** is generally required for loan approval.
- ❑ **If the vested accrued benefit = $20,000 or less:**

    - You are not taxed on the loan, when added to all other outstanding loans amounts to $10,000 or less.
    - The maximum loan may not exceed 50% of your vested account balance. The Labor Department only allows up to 50% of the vested balance to be 1used as loan security. If additional collateral is provided, loans in excess of the 50% cap are allowed.

- ❑ **If the vested accrued benefit is greater than $20,000:**

    - You will not be taxed on a loan that does not exceed the lesser of $50,000 or 50% of the vested benefit, as long as you did not borrow from any employer plan within a one-year period ending on the day before the date of the new loan.
    - If you borrowed within the one-year period, the $50,000 limit will be further reduced. The maximum loan limit is calculated by the difference between highest outstanding balance of all loans during the one-year period ending the day before the new loan and the outstanding balance of the participant's loans from the plan on the date of the new loan.

INTEREST DEDUCTION LIMITATIONS

If you are not a key employee and want to borrow from your account to purchase a first or second residence, you can generally obtain a full interest deduction by using the residence as collateral for the loan. Your account balance may not be used to secure the loan. Interest deductions for plan loans are not allowed for key employees

If you are not a key employee and use the plan for investment purposes, and the loan is not secured by your elective deferrals or allocable income to a 401k plan, the loan account interest is deductible up to investment income. Unless your residence is the security for the loan, interest on loans used for personal purposes is not deductible.

LOANS FROM 401K PLANS

The rules governing loans from 401k plans are the same as those discussed above. It should be noted that all participants, not just owners, are prohibited from deducting interest on plan loans. However, the interest is really being paid to the participant's own account, so the loss of a deduction is not as important.

For more information see: *IRS Publication 575*

WITHDRAWALS

Amounts attributable to elective deferrals and qualified non-elective deferrals may not be distributed earlier than:

- ❏ Separation from service (termination, discharge, death or disability).
- ❏ Termination of the plan without the establishment or maintenance of another defined contribution plan (except an ESOP).
- ❏ The attainment of age 59 ½ (profit sharing and stock bonus plans only).
- ❏ Hardship of the employee.

HARDSHIP WITHDRAWALS

While hardship withdrawals are permitted, there are some rules and employer must follow if permitting the withdrawals. First, the plan documents must permit hardship withdrawals. Second, the amount of hardship withdrawal is limited to the employee's deferral amounts, generally without earnings. Third, they may be made under the following conditions:

- ❑ It is not permissible to withdraw employer contributions in a hardship withdrawal,
- ❑ A hardship distribution is limited to the amount that will satisfy an immediate and financial need of the employee. IRS regulation states that an immediate and heavy financial need is:

  - Expenses for medical care (as defined in IRC §213(d) previously incurred by the employee or his or her spouse or dependents or necessary for these persons to obtain medical care,
  - Costs directly related to the purchase of a principal residence for the employee (excluding mortgage payments),
  - Payment of tuition, related educational fees, and room and board expenses for the next 12 months of post-secondary education for the employee or the employee's spouse, children or dependents, or
  - Payment necessary to prevent the eviction of the employee from his or her principal residence or foreclosure on the mortgage of the employee's principal residence.

IN-SERVICE DISTRIBUTIONS

The law will allow you to take distributions in very limited circumstances from your profit sharing plan while your business is still in operation. The limited circumstances under which you can take in-service distributions are the following:

- ❑ A distribution to a participant after he or she has participated in the plan for a fixed number of years, usually at least two.

❑ A distribution after the participant attains a stated age. (The age is generally set by the plan.)
❑ A distribution to a participant upon the occurrence of some event, such as layoff, illness, disability, retirement, death or termination of employment.
❑ In-Service Distributions are generally not a taxable event if the distribution is done to rollover your funds into another qualified plan.

EARLY DISTRIBUTIONS AND EXCEPTIONS

Any distribution (other than a rollover) you take from your profit sharing plan before you reach age 59 ½ is considered an early distribution, which means you must pay a 10% penalty in addition to income tax unless an exception applies. The exceptions will eliminate the penalty, but not the income tax. Exceptions include:

❑ **Death:** Distribution from your profit sharing plan after you die is not subject to the early distribution penalty, no matter how old you are when you die or how old your beneficiaries are when they withdraw the money.
❑ **Disability:** If you become disabled, you can take money from your profit sharing plan without penalty. But first you must satisfy the IRS's definition of disabled, which can be difficult. It reads: "You must be unable to engage in any substantial gainful activity by reason of any medical determinable physical or mental impairment which can be expected to result in death or to be of long-continued and indefinite duration." The IRS's own regulations state that the gainful activity refers specially to the type of work you were doing before becoming disabled. Thus it would seem that you need not be unfit for all work; just the work you customarily do.
❑ **Periodic Payments:** You can begin taking distributions from your self-employed plan regardless of your age as

51

long as you take them in equal annual installments over your life expectancy.

❑ **Leaving Your Business after Age 55:** If you are at least 55 years old when you leave or terminate your business, any distributions you receive from your profit sharing plan will not be subject to an early distribution penalty.

❑ **QDRO Payments:** If you are paying child support or alimony from your retirement plan, or if you intend to distribute some or the entire plan to your former spouse as part of a property settlement, none of those payments are subject to the early distribution penalty as long as there is a QDRO in place that orders the payments. (See Section 4, above, for more information about QDROs).

❑ **Refunds:** If you contributed more to your profit sharing plan than you were permitted to deduct during the year, generally you can remove the excess without penalty if you do so before you file your tax return.

❑ **Mandatory Distributions:** If you own your own business, you must start taking money out of your profit sharing plan beginning in the year you turn 72 even if you are still working. If you are still working when your reach 72, you may continue to make contributions to a profit sharing plan and deduct those contributions. It could very well make sense for you to do so even though you are also required to take some money out each year.

❑ **Medical Expenses:** Although you can take money out of your profit sharing plan prior to age 59 ½ to pay for medical expenses, you won't escape the penalty entirely. The exemption applies only to the portion of your medical expenses that would be deductible on Schedule A of your tax return if you were to itemize deductions (whether or not you actually do itemize deductions). The remainder is subject to penalty.

EXAMPLE: Your adjusted gross income of $50,000. You had medical bills of $6,000 during the year, which you paid with funds you withdrew from your profit sharing plan. (The $6,000 distribution is included in the $50,000 of income.) For income tax purposes, you are permitted to deduct medical expenses that exceed 7.5% of your adjusted gross income. Thus:

Adjusted gross income (AGI, including the profit sharing plan distribution = $50,000;
7.5% of AGI (.075 x $50,000) = $3,750 nondeductible expense;
Excess ($6,000 - $3,750) = $2,250 deductible expenses.

Although you took $6,000 from your profit sharing plan to pay medical expenses, only $2,250 will escape the early distribution penalty. The remaining $3,750 will be subject to the penalty (unless you qualify for another exception), and the entire $6000 is subject to regular income tax.

DIVORCE PAYMENTS

Congress has passed legislation to protect your self-employed plan assets. The key protection provision is known as the "anti-alienation" rule, which attempts to ensure that you (the plan participant) cannot voluntarily or involuntarily transfer your interest in plan assets to another person or entity. However, divorce is a unique situation. What if you must use your retirement plan as part of a property settlement? Can you transfer some or all of your interest in the plan assets in this situation? And if you can, who should be responsible for the taxes and penalties (if any) on the part you transfer?

Congress addressed these concerns by giving divorcing couples a vehicle for protecting plan assets and minimizing tax and penalties. It's called a Qualified Domestic Relations Order or QDRO. The QDRO rules spell out the circumstances under which your qualified plan benefits can go to someone else such as your soon-to-be former spouse. These rules also provide liability protection to the trustee who distributes the assets under the terms of the

QDRO. A QDRO is a judgment, decree, or order (including a court approved property settlement agreement) that satisfies all of the following requirements:

❑ It contains certain language, specifically:

- The alternate payee must be referred to as "the alternate payee" in the QDRO
- The QDRO must identify the plan, as well as the amount of each payment and the number of payments to be made.
- The QDRO must contain the name and address of both you and the alternate payee.

❑ It relates to child support, alimony or martial property rights of your spouse, dependent child or some other dependent.
❑ It gives an alternate payee, such as a spouse, former spouse, dependent child or other dependent, the right to receive all or a portion of your plan benefits.
❑ It does not alter the form or the amount of the benefit originally intended for you, even though the benefit might now go to an alternate payee. For example, the QDRO cannot require the plan to pay a larger annuity to the alternate payee than it would have paid to you.

If you have a QDRO in place, the law will allow the trustee of the plan to distribute to the alternate payee his or her share of you plan assets without disqualifying the plan-as long as the plan also permits distribution. And generally, he or she will be responsible for any income taxes on the distributions he or she receives.

INCLUDING EMPLOYEES IN YOUR PLAN

Your plan must include all employees who have at least one year of service and have reached age 21. In some cases, an employee may be required to complete two years of service before participating in your plan. You generally are not required to cover seasonal or part-time employees who work less than 1,000 hours during a 12-month period. A plan may not discriminate in favor of officers or other highly compensated personnel and may not exclude employees who are over a certain age. Benefits must be for the employees, their beneficiaries, and their plan rights may not be subject to forfeiture. A plan may not allow any of its funds to be diverted for purposes other than pension benefits.

ASSET PROTECTION

As mentioned previously, assets held in a qualified retirement plan are required to contain "anti alienation" provisions under ERISA. Therefore, pursuant to bankruptcy laws, employer and employee assets in qualified retirement plans are generally protected from creditors including the IRS. I recommend you discuss this with your tax advisor as every situation is different.

Where to Claim Deductions for Retirement Plans

EMPLOYEES

If you contribute to an IRA and are entitled to a deduction, you claim it on page one of Form 1040 as an adjustment to gross income. If you contribute to a salary reduction plan (such as a SIMPLE or a 401k plan), your contribution is reflected on your W-2 as a reduction of wages.

ALL EMPLOYERS

To claim the credit for plan start-up costs of small employers, file Form 8881 Credit for Small Employer Pension Plan Startup Costs.

SELF-EMPLOYED

Contributions you make to self-employed qualified retirement plans, SEPs, or SIMPLEs on behalf of your employees are entered on Schedule C on the specific line provided on the form called, pension and profit-sharing plans. Contributions you make on your own behalf are claimed on page one of Form 1040 as an adjustment to gross income. Contributions you make to an IRA are also claimed on page one of Form 1040 as an adjustment to gross income.

PARTNERSHIPS AND LLCS

Deductions for contributions to qualified plans on behalf of employees are part of the partnership's or LLC's ordinary trade or business income on Form 1065. The deductions are entered on the line provided for retirement plans.

If partners and members set up qualified retirement plans, they claim deductions for their contributions on page one of Form 1040, as an adjustment to income. It is important to note that the entity does not make contributions on behalf of partners or members.

S CORPORATIONS

Deductions for contributions to qualified plans are taken by the corporation as part of its ordinary trade or business income on Form 1120S. Enter the deduction on the line provided for pension, profit-sharing, and other plans.

C CORPORATIONS

C Corporations deduct contributions to retirement plans on Form 1120. The deduction is entered on the line provided for pension, profit-sharing.

OTHER REPORTING REQUIREMENTS FOR ALL TAXPAYERS

Qualified plans have annual reporting requirements which state you must file certain information returns each year to report on the amount of plan assets, contributions, number of employees, and such (unless you are exempt from reporting). Information returns in the Form 5500 series are not filed with the IRS. Instead, these returns are filed with the Department of Labor's Pension and Welfare Benefits Administration (PWBA). With the exception of one person plans, all plans must file Form 5500, Annual Return/Report of Employee Benefit Plan each year. The return is due by the last day of the seventh month following the close of the plan year (July 31 for a calendar year plan).

Single participant plans are automatically exempt from annual reporting if the plan assets at the end of the year are $250,000 or less.

Form 1099R and Form 945 are also required for participant distributions.

Permitted Investments

Here is a list of some examples of what you can use your eQRP to invest in:

- ❑ Real Estate
- ❑ Gold Bullion coins and bars must be .9999 fine or US Eagles
- ❑ Silver Bullion coins and bars must be .999 fine
- ❑ U.S. Treasury Gold and Silver Coins
- ❑ Bitcoin and other crypto
- ❑ Small business start ups
- ❑ Tax Lien Certificates
- ❑ Trust Deeds
- ❑ Mortgage Notes
- ❑ Single and Multi-Family Residential Property
- ❑ Securities
- ❑ CD's
- ❑ Stocks
- ❑ Bonds
- ❑ Mutual Funds
- ❑ LLC's
- ❑ Apartment Buildings
- ❑ Co-Ops
- ❑ Condominiums
- ❑ Commercial Property
- ❑ Joint Ventures
- ❑ Improved or Unimproved Land
- ❑ Commodities
- ❑ Futures
- ❑ Contracts of Sale
- ❑ Factoring
- ❑ Like and Unlike Exchanges
- ❑ Leases
- ❑ Palladium.
- ❑ Life Insurance

LIFE INSURANCE

Life insurance can be purchased within an eQRP. Life Insurance is not allowed in an IRA. Life insurance must be "incidental" to the main retirement purpose of the plan, so there are limits on the amount of life insurance that can be purchased on behalf of a plan participant. These rules are different for defined benefit plans and defined contribution plans. Under a defined benefit plan, the face amount of insurance generally cannot exceed 100 times the participant's projected monthly retirement benefit.

Example: If the projected monthly retirement benefit were $4,000, the limit on the life insurance that could be provided would be $400,000. Coverage in excess of this amount would not be deemed "incidental."

http://www.eegroup.com/life_ins_in_qual_plan.html

WHO MAY BE INVOLVED IN YOUR INVESTMENT DECISION?

The following may be involved with your transaction along with you:

- ❑ Participants in the Qualified Plan
- ❑ Accountant
- ❑ Attorney or Escrow Agent
- ❑ Financial Advisor
- ❑ Lender(s)
- ❑ Partners
- ❑ Seller
- ❑ Trustee or Custodian and/or Administrator/Record Keeper

DISALLOWED ASSETS:

Anything considered a collectible, such as:

- ❏ Art
- ❏ Rugs
- ❏ Stamp or Collectible Coins (certain bullion coins are allowed, as specified above)
- ❏ Metal or Gem
- ❏ Antiques

REAL ESTATE

You can invest and hold almost any type of real estate you'd like with your eQRP other then a property that you or a disqualified party receive any current benefit from.

For Example you can buy a vacation house in San Diego to rent out but you can't use it one weekend a year and then rent it out the rest of the time. This would be considered receiving a current benefit from it.

The IRS does not permit active investments inside a qualified plan. This means you can't buy a property, spend a bunch of time fixing it up and then selling it and deferring the gains and income inside your plan. The IRS looks at that type of activity and calls it a business or trade and imposes a 35% tax through UBIT (Unrelated Business Income Tax). We've heard of people getting away with doing this, adding a little bit of work here and there but you're better off staying very black and white. See *Internal Revenue Code § 4975*

If you buy a property stick with those that are professionally managed. The truth is that the property should be able to support professional property management anyway. If it can't survive financially without you doing all the work, you may want to rethink investing in it in the first place.

If you do want to buy a property and do the work yourself, consider doing the investment inside a corporation or LLC enjoying the tax advantages there, not risking the violation of running an active business inside a qualified plan.

The law allows you to contribute a certain amount of money to your plan each year, lets say that amount is $20,500. If you spent 500 hours doing labor doing work to the property you're really contributing another $5000, $10,000 or more depending on what that labor time would have cost on the open market. You've effectively back-door contributed to your plan above the limits the government set. We don't recommend doing this.

Your eQRP is allowed to take out debt, called qualified debt, to purchase a property but the debt is required to be non-recourse, meaning neither you nor the eQRP can guarantee it. The property is the only thing that can be used for collateral or as a guarantee. You generally do not have limits on the amount of debt relative to the property and will not have problems with UDFI (unrelated debt financed income) or UBIT, (unrelated business income tax) when you use debt on property inside your eQRP.

Unfortunately IRA's are not exempt from UDFI and profits from an investment using debt that an IRA makes would be forced to pay the penalty. Any real estate investor should think twice before investing their retirement money in real estate with debt because of the penalty.

For this reason alone the eQRP is vastly superior to the IRA for a real estate investor.

PRECIOUS METALS - Gold, Silver & Platinum

The eQRP is unique in it's ability for an owner of the plan or anyone else to be trustee and manage account assets. (see: USC § 403b) This includes deciding on the facility to store precious metals so long as they are managed with reasonable care and no disqualified party receives current benefit. (see ERISA 29 USC § 1103) You couldn't receive the bullion and turn it into jewelry for example. This would be considered receiving a current benefit.

As a trustee you are in a fiduciary role to protect the assets so if your plan buys gold you'd be violating your responsibilities as a fiduciary if you buried the assets in your back yard.

Holding the assets of the plan in a bank safety deposit box or in a vault at home is reasonable and should cause no problems with the IRS or Department of Labor in terms of custody and care of assets.

> **WARNING: IRA's are vastly different than the eQRP because USC § 408 requires an IRA custodian of assets to be a bank or non-bank custodian. A non-bank custodian must seek approval by the IRS. Any type of self directed IRA that suggest you can avoid this custodian requirement by setting up a shell company that takes ownership of metals is likely jeopardizing the assets of the IRA should the IRS find out. This is a case of the form of the structure satisfies the USC § 408 but the substance of the structure does not and is therefore a violation in the Department of Labor and IRS' eyes.**

The following gold, silver, platinum and palladium are permissible. There may be more but these clearly fall into the permissible category given the IRS and DOL guidelines as of 2012

❑ Acceptable Gold Coins (31 USC § 5112):

- US Minted Eagles of any size
- US Minted Buffalos
- Austrian Philharmonic Coins, Australian Kangaroo and Nuggets, Kookaburras and Koala Coins
- Canadian Maple Leaf Coins, any size
- Gold bars and rounds manufactured by a NYMEX or COMEX approved refiner/assayer and meeting minimum fineness requirements of .995+; most gold bullion bars are 99.99% pure, what the industry calls "four 9s gold." as described in section 7 of the Commodity Exchange Act, 7 USC 7
- Investors with large eQRP's should consider the ten-ounce and the kilo bars (32.15 ounces) because the larger bars carry smaller markups over spot. As a rule, the larger the bar, the smaller the markup

❑ Acceptable Silver Coins (31 USC § 5112):

- US Minted Eagles
- Canadian Maple Leafs
- Silver Mexican Libertads
- Silver bars and rounds manufactured by a COMEX approved refiner/assayer and meeting minimum fineness requirements of .999+ as described in section 7 of the Commodity Exchange Act, 7 USC 7

❑ Acceptable Platinum

- Canadian Maple Leafs
- Platinum bars and rounds manufactured by a NYMEX approved refiner/assayer and meeting minimum fineness requirements of .9995+, as described in section 7 of the Commodity Exchange Act, 7 USC 7

❑ Acceptable Palladium

- Canadian Maple Leafs
- Platinum Isle of Man Noble Coins
- Palladium bars and rounds manufactured by a NYMEX approved refiner/assayer and meeting minimum fineness requirements of .9995+, as described in section 7 of the Commodity Exchange Act, 7 USC 7

Disallowed Investments & Prohibited Transactions

DISALLOWED INVESTMENTS

Collectibles

For purposes of this subsection, the term "collectible" means:

- ❑ Any work of art
- ❑ Any rug or antique or autos
- ❑ Any metal or gem
- ❑ Any stamp or coin
- ❑ Any other tangible personal property specified by the Secretary of the Department of Labor for purposes of this subsection

PROHIBITED TRANSACTIONS

A prohibited transaction is any improper or illegal use of a qualified plan by the plan participant or any disqualified person. If you or your beneficiary engages in a prohibited transaction (as defined under Section 4975 of the Internal Revenue Code), the plan **could lose its tax exemption** and you must include the value of your account in your gross income for that taxable year.

You are a disqualified person if you are:

- ❑ An employer of any of the participants in the plan
- ❑ A 10% (or greater) partner in a partnership that has the plan
- ❑ A fiduciary of the plan (including yourself and any advisors)
- ❑ A highly compensated partner (an employee who makes 10% or more of the employer's annual wages)

❑ An employee organization with any participating members who are covered by the plan
❑ A person providing services to the plan
❑ If you are a disqualified person, your related persons will also be disqualified persons. These related persons include members of the plan owner's family such as:

- Spouses, ancestors, direct descendants and any spouses of direct descendants
- Corporations, partnerships, trusts or estates in which you own, directly or indirectly, at least half of the total voting stock or the value of all stock of a corporation, beneficial interest of the trust or estate
- Capital interest or profit interest in the partnership

PROHIBITED TRANSACTIONS BETWEEN DISQUALIFIED PERSONS:

❑ A transfer of plan income or assets to, or use of plan income or assets by, or for the benefit of, a disqualified person, is a prohibited transaction.
❑ Dealing with plan income or assets by a fiduciary for his or her own interest is a prohibited transaction.
❑ The receiving of consideration by a fiduciary for his or her own account from a party that is dealing with the plan in a transaction that involves plan income or assets is prohibited transaction.

Prohibited Transactions between the plan and disqualified person:

❑ Selling, exchanging or leasing property
❑ Lending money or extending credit
❑ Furnishing goods, services or facilities

AVOIDING PROHIBITED TRANSACTIONS

The following are acts that you should avoid:

- ❑ Improper use of your Qualified Plan Assets by you or any disqualified person
- ❑ Borrowing money from it and not following prescribed regulations
- ❑ Selling property to it
- ❑ Using it as security for a loan

EXEMPTIONS

A prohibited transaction does not take place if you are a disqualified person and receive any benefit to which you are entitled to as a plan participant or beneficiary. However, the benefit must be calculated and paid under the same terms as all other participants and beneficiaries.

The same transaction involving a 401k plan

The purchase of a property in a 401k Plan is as straightforward as making the purchases personally. The only difference is that there is an intermediary, such as a trustee or a Third Party Administrator (TPA) performing the transaction on behalf of your Profit Sharing 401k Plan. In many cases this person is the owner of the business.

Unrelated business income tax on debt financed property involving a qualified plan

In many circumstances, UDFI does not apply to income from debt financed property in a qualified plan. There is a limited exception in the definition of acquisition indebtedness contained in section 514(c)(9) of the Internal Revenue Code for plans under section 401, including profit sharing, 401k plan, and defined benefit plans. For more information on this exemption, please see your tax advisor.

Establishing An eQRP

The first step in setting up a qualified retirement plan is to establish a written plan, which fulfills the requirements of the IRS. The written plan must be adopted by the last day of the tax year in which the employer starts the plan. The employer is then required to communicate the specifics of the plan to eligible employees. The basic steps in setting up a qualified retirement plan are easy and usually take less then 3 business days.

1. Fill out the 1 page information sheet at www.eqrp.co and submit on-line OR call 800-270-1649
2. Our office will then prepare the complete set of plan documents and email them for your eSignature. We will also include your new **Federal Identification Number.**
3. Your bank account will be ready within 2 days.
4. If you have employees, let them know of the plan specifics and options.
5. Rollover IRAs and other qualified plan assets to your new plan.
6. You can now make deductible plan contributions and elective deferrals (401k) to your new plan
7. Invest the plan assets.

Qualified Plan Administration

In addition to the requirements for establishing a qualified retirement plan, employers are responsible for operating the plan on an ongoing basis. After the qualified retirement plan is established, the employer, trustee or plan administrator is responsible for operational and administrative duties. These administrative responsibilities include:

Making contributions in accordance with the plan.

❑ Keeping the plan up-to-date and in compliance with all retirement plan laws.
❑ Investing the plan assets.
❑ Providing information and required disclosure to plan participants.
❑ Distributing benefits in accordance with the plan.
❑ Informing eligible employees about in the plan.

INFORMATION RETURNS

Qualified plan administrators must also file Form 5500, *Annual Return/Report of Employee Benefit Plan*, annually with the IRS.

Form 5500-EZ, *Annual Return of One-Participant (Owners and Their Spouses) Retirement Plan*, is a short-form information return that is filed by pension plans, profit-sharing plans, and 401k plans that cover:

❑ Only owners or an individual and his or her spouse who wholly own the trade or business for which the plan is established.
❑ Only partners and their spouses in a business partnership for which the plan is established.

Form 5500-EZ must be filed annually. However, some plans having $250,000 or less in total assets at the close of the plan's accounting year do not have to file. According to the instructions for both Form 5500 and 5500-EZ, each form is due by the last day of the seventh calendar month after the end of the plan year.

Tax Alerts

Using Your Retirement Plan as a Tax Shelter

A single person eQRP 401k plan can be a nice tax shelter for proprietors, who as individuals can contribute a maximum of $20,500 if under 50 years of age or $27,000 as elective deferrals if age 50 or older for 2022. Also, your firm can contribute an additional 20% of net earnings (minus your elective deferral contribution). So on $100,000 of net earning, you can put away around $35,000 into an eQRP another $6500 if over 50. The maximum total contribution for 2022 is $61,000 ($67,500 if over 50 years for 2022).

Also under the microscope: Seniors with regular IRAs.

The IRS believes many people age 72 and over don't take required minimum payouts. It plans to scrutinize Forms 5498 filed by IRA trustees to spot potential problems. IRS will notify delinquents, requesting them to take catch-up distributions, according to Hawes, CPA.

Penalties for Failure to Report or Disclose

Plan administrators, employers, and other parties are liable for penalties for failing to comply with reporting and disclosure rules. The IRS imposes a penalty of $25 per day (up to $15,000) for not filing returns in connection with pension, profit-sharing, and other retirement plans by the required due date.

The Department of Labor may assess a civil penalty of up to $1,100 per day against a plan administrator from the date of the administrator's failure or refusal to file an annual report until the report is filed.

What are the advantages of a Qualified Retirement Plan over an IRA?

	Qualified Plan	**IRA**
Can you borrow from your retirement account?	YES- Permitted up to $50,000 or ½ vested account	Not Allowed
Debt financing on real estate without adverse tax consequences?	Permitted	Not permitted
Deductible contribution limit for 2022?	$61,000 for 401k, profit sharing and $245,000 for defined benefit plan	Only $6000
Protection from creditors in lawsuits?	YES-ERISA provided protection	No-ERISA protection
Protection from creditors in Bankruptcy?	YES-ERISA provided protection	Minimal and subjective
Ability to purchase life insurance?	YES	Not permitted
Ability to be your own trustee, write and sign checks, and directly control your plan assets?	YES	Not permitted
Employee contribution (elective deferrals)	$20,500	Not Permitted
Catch up contributions if over age 50	$ 6,500	$1,000

The 8th Wonder of the World

Compound interest is the eighth wonder of the world. He who understands it, earns it ... he who doesn't ... pays it.

- Albert Einstein

The inverse of that is taxation, possibly the most destructive force on wealth ever.

Saving cash, you get taxed each year for the money as it comes out of your paycheck, and all the interest earned on that money. Tax deferral, or using your eQRP to take money out to your paycheck pre-tax, you are not taxed as the money grows in the account but will be taxed when the money is taken out

Tax Avoidance, or ROTH eQRP is paying the taxes up front for the principal amount, but the interest earned is never taxed.

Section 2

eQRP vs. et.al

What are the advantages of the eQRP vs. an IRA?

❑ With the EQRP, you can be the trustee which means you make all the investment decision, write/sign checks, and have full control of the plan.
❑ You cannot be the trustee of an IRA.

IRS Publication 590 clearly states the following in regard to an IRA:

> *"An individual retirement account (IRA) is a trust or custodial account set up in the United States for the exclusive benefit of you or your beneficiaries. The account is created by a written document. The document must show that the account meets all of the following requirements. The trustee or custodian must be a bank, a federally insured credit union, a savings and loan association, or an entity approved by the IRS to act as trustee or custodian…"*

-Source: *IRS Publication 590*

❑ You can borrow money from your eQRP. You can borrow up to $50,000 or ½ your vested account balance, whichever is less, from your EQRP. You cannot borrow from an IRA.
❑ Under ERISA laws, the eQRP has protection from creditors, IRS, and bankruptcy. An IRA has limited if any protections from creditors the IRS or bankruptcy.
❑ Contribution limits for the eQRP in 2022 are $61,000 ($20,500 individual + company contributions) annually. You can only contribute $6000 to an IRA in 2022.
❑ The eQRP allows you to purchase life insurance. You cannot purchase life insurance with an IRA.

- The eQRP allows employees to make elective deferrals of up to $20,500 in 2022. IRA does not allow elective deferrals.
- The EQRP allows catch up contributions of $6,500 if you are over 50 years old. An IRA only allows for $1,000 catch up contribution.
- The eQRP allows for hardship withdrawals and an IRA does not allow hardship withdrawals.
- The eQRP allows you to be a stockholder in a sub chapter S Corp and an IRA does not allow this.
- The eQRP allows you to leverage real estate without UBIT tax. IRA's get Slammed with UBIT tax when leverage is used.

Comparison of Qualified Retirement Plans

The different choices of qualified retirement plans have been discussed at length. But how do you know which plan is best for you? There are several factors to consider:

❑ **How much money do you have to set aside in a retirement plan?** If your business is continually profitable you may want to commit to a plan that requires contributions without regard to profits. If your business is good in some years but not in others, you may want to use a profit sharing plan that does not require contributions in less profitable years.

❑ **How much will it cost to cover employees?** When there are few or no employees, then the choice of plan is largely a question of what will be the most beneficial to you. When a large number of employees will use the plan, the cost may be too prohibitive to provide substantial retirement benefits. However, if your competitors offer plans to their employees, you may want to offer similar benefits as a means to retaining employees.

❑ **How soon do you expect to retire?** The closer you are to retirement, the more inclined you may be to use a defined benefit plan to contribute as much as possible.

COMPARISON OF QUALIFIED RETIREMENT PLANS 2022

Type of Plan	Maximum Contribution	Last Date for Contribution
IRA	$6000 or taxable compensation, whichever is smaller ($7,000 for those 50 or older)	Due date of your return (without extensions)
SIMPLE plan	$14,000 (not to exceed taxable compensation), plus $3000 (catch-up contributions	Due date of employer's return for employer contributions (including extensions);
SEP-IRA	$61,000 or 20 % of participant's taxable compensation, whichever is smaller	Due date of employer's return (including extensions)
Defined Contribution Plans	Smaller of $61,000 (2022) or 25% of compensation (20% of self-employed income). Plus catch up contribution of $6500.	Due date of employer's return (including extensions) Note: Plan must be set up no later than the last day of the employer's tax year.
Defined Benefit Plan	Amount needed to provide provide retirement benefit no larger than the lesser of $245,000 (2022) or 100% of the participant's average taxable compensation for highest three consecutive years.	Due date of employer's return (including extension) but not later than the minimum funding deadline. Note: Plan must be set up no later than the last day of the employer's tax year.

EXHIBIT 1

Comparison of Plan Types and Uses –
Tax-Deferred and Tax-Free Investing (2022)

OBJECTIVES IN A TAX-DEFERRED PLAN?	Profit Sharing/401k	Simplified Employee Pension Plan	SIMPLE	IRA
As an employer, do you want to be able to contribute up to 25% of compensation for a given year?	YES To a maximum of $61,000	YES To a maximum of $61,000	YES To a maximum of $14,000	Maximum by law
As an employee, do you want to defer up to 100% of compensation?	Yes To a maximum of $20,500 plus catch-up provision of $6000 (Not counted as part of the 25% of your employer contribution)	Not Available	To a maximum of $14,000 plus catch-up provision.	Not Applicable
Do you want to self-direct all of your investments?	YES	YES – but most use a 3rd party	YES – but most use a 3rd party	YES – but most use a 3rd party
Do you want to be your own Trustee, Custodian and Administrator? For Example: Write and sign checks, sign all documents and / or take possession of Plan assets for; your account?	YES, or you may appoint others for each of these roles	Not Permitted by Law	Not Permitted by Law	Not Permitted by Law

Do you want to borrow from your Retirement Account?	YES, Up to a maximum of $50,000 of your vested Account Balance	Not Permitted by Law	Not Permitted by Law	Not Permitted by Law
Do you want to retire before age 59 ½ and receive distributions penalty free?	YES, age 55 is an acceptable retirement age	59 ½ is the earliest, without substantially equal periodic payments	59 ½ is the earliest, without substantially equal periodic payments	59 ½ is the earliest, without substantially equal periodic payments
Do you want to make sure that your assets are protected from creditors?	YES, Your benefits are not accessible to creditors, as ERISA provided for your benefits to be "Non-alienable"	No anti-alienation provision exists, but many states protect a portion of assets	No anti-alienation provision exists, but many states protect a portion of assets	No anti-alienation provision exists, but many states protect a portion of assets
Do you want Life Insurance as part of your retirement portfolio?	YES	Prohibited	Prohibited	Prohibited
Do you want to be able to make "in kind" contributions of assets that you own, not just cash?	YES, provided that you have no common law employees, and the Plan covers you, your spouse and partners only.	Not Permitted	Not Permitted	Not Permitted

Note: self-employed individuals take into account the deductions allowed for one-half of the self-employment tax and contributions to the plan

EXHIBIT 2

Retirement Plan Limits 2021 vs. 2022

For most of the retirement plan limits, the cost-of-living index increased enough to trigger their adjustment. For example, the maximum annual contribution to 401k, 403(b) and 457 plans, which adjusted in $500 increments, is $20,500 in 2022. Some of the other limits were adjusted as well. IRA contribution limits, which were established by EGTRRA, remain at $6000, plus $1,000 catch-up for people over 50.

For More Information See: IRS Publication IR-2012-77

	2021	2022
Maximum annual benefit under a defined -benefit plan	$230,000	$245,000
Maximum annual contribution for defined-contribution plans	$58,000	$61,000
Annual Compensation limit used for determining retirement plan contributions	$290,000	$305,000
Maximum annual contribution to 401k, 403(b), and 457 plans	$19,500	$20,500
Catch-up contribution for individuals age 50 or over	$6,500	$6,500
Maximum annual SIMPLE employee deferral	$13,500	$14,000
SIMPLE catch-up deferral-age 50 or over	$3,000	$3,000
SEP minimum compensation	$650	$650
Maximum annual IRA contribution	$6,000	$6,000
Catch-up IRA contribution	$1,000	$1,000

Income of key employee in top-heavy plan	$185,000	$200,000
Definition of highly compensated employee	$130,000	$135,000
Social Security wage base (OASDI only; no limit for Medicare)	$142,800	$147,000
Social Security tax rate (employee)	7.65%	7.65%
Social Security tax rate (self-employed)	15.30%	15.30%

Section 3

The Rabbit
The Rollover Side Hustle eQRP

You're either an employee or you might be retired with an old 401k, 403b or 457 account from a previous employer. Your retirement money may still be with the previous plans administrator or you may have rolled it into an IRA. (an IRA that was created from doing a rollover of a 401k, 403b or 457 is called a **Conduit IRA**)

What you want:

You want to invest your retirement account in alternative investments like Bitcoin, gold, silver, real estate, private lending etc. instead of the typical "faulty five" pack offered by many employers' 401k. The faulty five often look like a selection of investments:

- ❏ Money Market Fund
- ❏ Bond Fund
- ❏ Small Cap Stock Fund
- ❏ Big Cap Stock Fund
- ❏ International Fund

What you really want is the ability to invest in assets like:

- ❏ Gold and Silver Bars and coins
- ❏ Bitcoin
- ❏ Real Estate, domestic and international
- ❏ Land
- ❏ Commercial paper, including mortgages
- ❏ Private businesses
- ❏ Stocks, Bonds and Mutual funds
- ❏ Foreign Currencies

- ❏ Private placements
- ❏ Tax liens

With your Rollover Side Hustle eQRP you can invest in all these things and more. The IRS only disallows certain things as investments and certain persons from being a part of the transaction.

Disallowed Investments and Disqualified Persons

The Internal Revenue Code does not describe what the eQRP can invest in, only what it cannot invest in. Internal Revenue Code Section 4975 prohibits Disqualified Persons from engaging in certain type of transactions. The purpose of these rules is to encourage the use of retirement funds for accumulation and prohibit those in control of retirement funds from taking advantage of the tax benefits for their personal account. For a full list of disallowed items and the definition of a Disqualified Person, see this section (In the Definitions section)

Rabbit Action Plan:

1. **Apply for your eQRP** by filling out the app at eQRP.co or calling 800-270-1649. 48 hours later you'll receive your trust docs. Review them and you're ready to fund:
2. **Rollover.** The eQRP company will work with your current custodian to transfer funds and assets from your old plan to your eQRP. Any qualified account that can be rolled over into your eQRP is done tax free and penalty free in every case.
3. **Contribute.** Start contributing as much as you can directly from your paycheck. Any contributions must be direct withdrawals from wages or earnings and transferred from your business account to the eQRP account. You are not permitted to deposit personal funds into your eQRP account.

4. **Invest**. Invest in whatever you'd like: as long as you're investing in an allowed investment and not something disqualified or with a disqualified person you can write the check for the investment.

5. **Management**: Keep up with the bookkeeping on anything your eQRP does. The IRS requires basic record keeping. You can also hire a bookkeeper, accountant or third party to do this very inexpensively.

Just because you didn't have an active business at the time of set up doesn't mean you can't contribute down the road if and when you start making money as a consultant or through services you directly perform.

TIP: passive income is not eligible to contribute to your eQRP, it must be active income.

Section 4

The Squirrel

The eQRP for the Unicorn Single Operator

aka the Energetic eQRP

An eQRP for the self-employed person or small business owner with no other employees. It offers powerful features not found in traditional 401k or IRA retirement plans.

The Presence of Self-Employment Activity

Self-Employment activity generally includes ownership and operation of a Sole Proprietorship, Limited Liability Company (LLC), C Corporation, S Corporation or a Limited Partnership where the business intends to generate revenue for profit and make contributions to the plan. Once the company is created, there must be income based on the work of those entities to contribute to the retirement plan. Any contributions must be derived from earned income reported on a W-2 subject to self-employment tax.

Generating Revenue for Profit

There are no established thresholds for how much profit the business must generate, how much money must be contributed to the plan, or how soon profits and contributions must happen. It's generally believed that the IRS will consider the business eligible if it is conducting legitimate business that is run with the intention of generating profits. The self-employment activity can be part time and it can be ancillary to the owners full or part time employment elsewhere.

Why an eQRP?

In 2022 you can contribute $20,500 as your employee elective deferral contribution. An additional $6500 can be contributed if you are over 50, called a Catch-Up Contribution.

Through your role of employer (which is your own company or simply you if you're a sole proprietor you can contribute up to $40,500 each year as the profit-sharing component).

If a business owner's spouse elects to participate in the eQRP and earns compensation from the business, the spouse is allowed to make separate and equal contributions increasing the couple's annual total contribution up to $122,000 or $135,000 if both spouses are over age 50.

Checkbook Control

An eQRP allows you, the owner, to choose any person you'd like to be the trustee, including yourself. The trustee is responsible for writing checks for investments. This is where Checkbook Control comes from. As trustee of the plan, you no longer have to get each and every investment you'd like to make approved by an outside custodian or trustee. If you want to invest it's as simple writing a check.

This control means all assets of your eQRP trust are under your sole authority. It also means you eliminate the expense and delays associated with a custodian like you're required to have with an IRA. This enables you to act quickly when the right investment presents itself to you.

USC §408 requires all IRA's to have a bank or approved non-bank custodian.

ALERT: Effective November 2021 Checkbook IRA's are now illegal. The McNalty v. Commissioner ruling disallowed the IRA checkbook LLC that promoters claimed got around the requirement.

The court ruled that the IRA owner can no longer be the one commanding the assets.

Just because some people may be getting away with this rule doesn't mean the activity is allowed. Be warned, this is a dangerous game to play and the penalty is up to 115% of assets that are part of any scheme to violate the rules or that involve prohibited transactions.

Administration, Maintenance and Compliance

Operating the eQRP is as simple as writing checks and keeping a basic accounting of what the plan has invested in, expenses of the plan and any revenue the plan earns. Most of the administration is keeping good records of investment activities, receipts and statements. Once the plan has more than $250,000 in assets, you're required to file a short form with the IRS, (Form 5500EZ can be filed online if you have less than $250,000 in assets in the plan).

Rollover Options

You are permitted to rollover any investment money from a previous employer's 401k, 403b or 457 or other qualified money like from an IRA or SEP. You're allowed to transfer those funds and assets into your eQRP. If you previously rolled over a 401k, 403b or 457 into an IRA you can do another rollover from the IRA into your eQRP. This type of IRA is classified as a Conduit IRA. All of these types of rollovers should be tax free and penalty free.

Make sure you transfer the funds directly from the trustee to trustee in order to avoid the 20% withholding requirement.

You can roll over as many different accounts as you'd like and consolidate them into your eQRP as long as they're qualified accounts like 401k, 403b, 457's, IRA's etc. Consolidating all these funds should save you money and time managing the funds and investing. It's a good idea to keep these funds in different checking accounts once you roll them into your eQRP. Please call us for further details about the various structures that might necessitate separate checking accounts.

Example 1 - Solo owner of a Corporation under age 50

Peter is 30 and the sole owner of Peters Pickles Inc. Peter receives $100,000 in compensation from the corporation. In 2022 the maximum contribution Peter can make to his eQRP account is $40,375. This is $20,500 from his elective employee contribution and $19,875 from his employer profit sharing portion. The $19,875 employer contribution is 25% of his taxable wages beyond his elective deferral.

$40,375 is significantly more than Peter would be able to contribute to a traditional plan or a SEP IRA.

Married

If Peter marries his girlfriend Patty and she starts earning wages from the company she can contribute up to $20,500 from her earnings and 25% of her wages can be contributed from the employer profit sharing.

Example 2 - Sole proprietor under age 50
(also applies to owners of an LLC)

Peter is 30 and does consulting for Pickle makers. Peter receives $100,000 in compensation from his consulting work. In 2022 the maximum deductible employee deferral contribution Peter can make to his EQRP account is $35,184. This is $20,500 from his elective employee contribution and $14,684 from his employer profit sharing portion. The $14,684 employer contribution is 20% of his taxable wages (after deducting his the elective deferral and half of self employment taxes), the maximum allowed for an LLC or sole proprietorship. If Peter formed an LLC for this work, he would still have a maximum employer contribution of $14,684, primarily because in a one person LLC the IRS considers this a "pass through, disregarded entity" and is looked at like a sole proprietorship for tax purposes.

$35,684 is significantly more than Peter would be able to contribute to a traditional plan or a SEP IRA.

Married

If Peter marries his girlfriend Patty and she starts earning wages from the company she can contribute up to $20,500 from her earnings and 20% of her wages can be contributed from the employer profit sharing.

Example 3 - Sole owner of a Corporation over age 50

Susan is 52 and the sole owner of Super Books Inc. Susan receives $150,000 in compensation from the corporation. In 2022 the maximum deductible employee deferral contribution Susan can make to her EQRP account is $57,750. This is $27,000 from her elective employee contribution plus $6500 extra for catch up since she's over 50 and $30,750 from her employer profit sharing portion. The $30,750 employer contribution is 25% of her taxable wages (above the 27,000 elective deferral contribution) . The maximum employer contribution from profit sharing is $30,750.

$57,750 is significantly more than Susan would be able to contribute to a traditional plan or a SEP IRA.

Married

If Susan's husband Sam, age 53 earns wages from the company he can contribute up to $27,000 from his earnings and 25% of his wages can be contributed from the employer profit sharing. If he earns $150,000 as well, he'll be able to contribute a total of $57,750 with a total between Sam and Susan of $115,500.

Example 4 - Sole Proprietor over age 50 (also applies to owners of an LLC)

Susan is 52 and writes Super Books as a freelance operator. Susan receives $100,000 in self-employment income from her work. In 2022 the maximum deductible employee deferral contribution Susan can make to her eQRP account is $40,483. This is $20,500 from her elective employee contribution plus $6500 extra for catch up since she's over 50 and $20,000 (20% of her taxable wages minus her $27,000 elective deferral and payroll taxes of 7.65%) from her employer profit sharing portion.

$40,483 is significantly more than Susan would be able to contribute to a traditional plan or a SEP IRA.

Married

If Susan's husband Sam, age 53, earns wages from the company he can contribute up to $27,000 from his earnings and 20% of his wages can be contributed from the employer profit sharing. Let's say he earns $80,000; he'll be able to contribute a total of $36,789. This is $27,000 from his employee deferral portion and $9,789 from his employer profit sharing contribution. The total between Sam and Susan in this example is $77,272.

The Roth Option:

In all the examples above the employee deferral contributions can be pretax or can be a Roth type contribution (contributed with after tax money). The profit-sharing employer contribution must be made as a pre-tax contribution.

The Loan -

With the eQRP you're permitted to borrow money from your plan for any purpose at any time. Pursuant to Internal Revenue Code Section 72(p), an eQRP loan is permitted at any time using the accumulated balance of the eQRP as collateral for the loan. The eQRP participant can borrow up to either $50,000 or 50% of their account value-whichever is less.

The loan must be repaid within 5 years and fully amortized within the chosen period of time with equal payments, no less then quarterly. The IRS requires a reasonable interest rate which generally means prime plus 1%. Prime in 2021 was around 3% so a minimum safe rate would be around 4%. Of course, if you paid a higher amount this would be one legal strategy to get more money into your plan in addition to the annual contributions.

Internal Revenue Code Section 72(p) and the 2001 EGTRRA law established the framework for the eQRP participant to borrow money from his eQRP account. As long as the plan documents allow for it and the proper loan documents are prepared and executed, a participant can borrow money for their eQRP account for any purpose. The eQRP loan is received tax-free and penalty-free. There are no penalties or taxes due provided the loan payments are paid on time. The eQRP documents you receive from the eQRP Company allow you to borrow money from your eQRP for any purpose, including real estate, funding your own business, paying off personal debt, going on vacation, etc.

The Ultimate Emergency Fund

Ever since the meltdown in 2008 banks have become more and more rigid about lending and have almost completely cut off lending to small businesses. The eQRP is a perfect structure for any self-employed business owner seeking immediate funds for their business without having to beg the bank.

Investment Options

The eQRP plan allows you to invest in almost any type of investment you can think of other then the small list of disallowed items and disqualified persons. Any income and gains from an investment are required to go directly back to your eQRP plan and flow back tax free.

Some of the options you may choose to invest in are:

- ❏ Gold and Silver Bars and coins* (see the metals supplement)
- ❏ Bitcoin
- ❏ Real Estate, domestic and international
- ❏ Land
- ❏ Commercial paper, including mortgages
- ❏ Private businesses
- ❏ Stocks, Bonds and Mutual funds
- ❏ Foreign Currencies
- ❏ Private placements
- ❏ Tax liens

Disallowed Investments and Disqualified Persons

The Internal Revenue Code does not describe what the eQRP can invest in, only what it cannot invest in. Internal Revenue Code Section 4975 prohibits Disqualified Persons from engaging in certain type of transactions. The purpose of these rules is to encourage the use of retirement funds for accumulation and prohibit those in control of retirement funds from taking advantage of the tax benefits for their personal account. For a full list of disallowed items and the definition of a Disqualified Person, see the section on DI's and DP's.

EGTRRA - Clarifying the eQRP for a self-employed person

In 2001, the Economic Growth and Tax Relief Reconciliation Act (EGTRRA) was passed. This act clarified how an eQRP could be used by a self-employed person who has no part time employees.* (Congress changed the rules in December 2019 changing the requirement from no full-time employees to no part time employees) to qualify for an individual 401k plan.

It also clarified that the self-employed eQRP participant can make contributions as both employee via elective deferral and employer via profit sharing. This dual contribution results in substantially higher limits then an IRA or other common vehicles.

SUMMARY

The eQRP is a highly flexible and tax-efficient retirement solution that will allow you to make high contributions to the plan either pre-tax or by designating it a ROTH and building part of it 100% tax free.

- ❑ Contribute up to $61,000 a year ($67,500 if you're over 50)
- ❑ Borrow up to $50,000 or 50% of your account value (whichever is less)
- ❑ Invest in almost any type of investment tax free including:

  - Precious metals like Gold, Silver and Platinum
  - Bitcoin
  - Real estate
  - Tax liens

- Private businesses
- Private loans
- Wall Street stuff like stocks and bonds

With the eQRP you're able to use your retirement funds to make almost any type of investment on your own without requiring the "consent" of anyone else like a custodian. The last thing you want is some technical bureaucrat telling you what you can or can't do with your own money, especially when the IRS has been very specific about what the rules are. Why would you limit your choices by working with a custodian? Plus, you have to pay fees to this person for the service of telling you no!!!

As a trustee of the eQRP, you will have "Checkbook Control" over the eQRP assets.

The eQRP allows you to invest tax free in an investment that you know and understand and even allows you to borrow up to $50,000 or 50% of the account for any purpose.

Aside from certain "prohibited transactions" involving Disqualified Persons, which are outlined in the Internal Revenue Code Section 4975, an eQRP can invest in most of the commonly made investments, including real estate, private business entities, public and private shares in companies and commercial and private paper.

Self-employed individuals: You can make contributions on behalf of yourself only if you have net earnings (Compensation) from self-employment in the trade or business for which the plan was set up. Your net earnings must be from your personal services, not from your investments. If you have a net loss from self-employment, you cannot make contributions for yourself for the year, even if you can contribute for common-law employees based on their compensation.

What if you have a job that offers a 401k or other retirement plan?

You can participate in an employer's 401k plan in tandem with your own eQRP. In that case the employee-elective deferrals from both plans are subject to the single contribution limit. ($20,500 in 2022 or $27,000 if over age 50) The maximum elective deferral contribution you can make as an employee, is $20,500 regardless of how many retirement plans you are involved in.

Employee Exemptions

Unlike the Honey Badger version of the eQRP that you'd likely set up as a Safe Harbor plan, a single person eQRP is for self-employed individuals or small business owners who have no employees and are not employed by any business owned by the individual or his/her spouse. (an exception applies if your full-time employee is your spouse). The business owners and their spouse are technically considered "owner-employees" rather than "employees."

The following types of employees may generally be excluded from coverage:

- ❑ Employees under 21 years of age
- ❑ Employees that work less than 500 hours annually
- ❑ Union Employees
- ❑ Nonresident alien employees
- ❑ Employees that have worked for you less than a year.

Once you have employees who qualify according to the terms above you can modify your plan very simply into a safe harbor plan. See the Honey Badger eQRP 401k chapter for details on this plan.

The conversion to the Safe Harbor plan is simple and can be done with one phone call and costs about $1500 to have all plan documents redone.

SQUIRREL ACTION PLAN:

1. **Apply for your eQRP** by filling out the app at eQRP.co or calling 800-270-1649. Within 48 hours you'll receive your trust docs. Review them and you're ready to fund:
2. **Rollover.** The eQRP company will work with your current custodian to transfer funds and assets from your old plan to your eQRP. Any qualified account that can be rolled over into your eQRP is done **tax free and penalty free in every case**.
3. **Contribute.** Start contributing as much as you can directly from your paycheck. Any contributions must be direct withdrawals from wages or earnings and transferred from your business account to the eQRP account. You are not permitted to deposit personal funds into your eQRP account.
4. **Invest.** Invest in whatever you'd like: as long as you're investing in an allowed investment and not something disqualified or with a disqualified person you can write the check for the investment.
5. **Management**: Keep up with the bookkeeping on anything your eQRP does. The IRS requires basic record keeping. You can also hire a bookkeeper, accountant or third party to do this very inexpensively.
6. **Convert.** When you hire any type of employee part time or full time, we recommend you contact the eQRP Company to modify your plan into a Safe Harbor™ eQRP.

Section 5

The Honey Badger eQRP 401k

Safe Harbor ™ eQRP plan for the Small-
Midsize Biz Owner with a team

aka the Safe Harbor eQRP 401k

A Safe Harbor eQRP 401k is designed for the small to mid-size business owner with 1-50 full time employees (not counting the owner and spouse). It offers powerful features not found in traditional 401k or IRA retirement plans.

Why a Safe Harbor eQRP 401k?

The Safe Harbor eQRP is a terrific way to defer up to $61,000 in wages ($67,500 if you're over age 50) every year. With a spouse you can defer double this amount. If you have a business with employees, this type of eQRP is an incentive to keep talented people and offers them a way to save and invest for their retirement.

Checkbook Control

A Safe Harbor eQRP 401k allows you, the owner, to choose any person you'd like to be the trustee. The trustee is responsible for writing checks for investments of the plan. This is where checkbook control comes from. As trustee of the plan, you no longer have to get each and every investment you'd like to make approved by an outside custodian or trustee. If you want to invest it's as simple as writing a check.

This control means all the assets of the eQRP trust are under your sole authority unless you employ an outside trustee to manage part of the assets. Many owners establish a relationship with a brokerage firm who offers wall street type investments, mutual funds, bond funds, etc. to the employees. This keeps the employer from having to manage and hold a bunch of different investments.

You are generally required to offer at least 3 investment options for your employees in addition to cash, anything beyond that is at you, the administrator's discretion.

Administration, Maintenance and Compliance

Operating the Safe Harbor eQRP 401k is as simple as writing checks and keeping a basic accounting of what the plan has invested in, expenses of the plan and any revenue the plan earns. Most of the administration is keeping good records of investment activities, receipts and statements. Once the plan has more than $250,000 in assets, you're required to file a short form with the IRS, (Form 5500).

Rollover Options

You are permitted to rollover any investment money from a previous employer's 401k, 403b or 457 or IRA with qualified money and transfer those funds and assets, no matter how many there are, into your eQRP. If you've already rolled over an old 401k, 403b or 457 into an IRA you can do another rollover from the IRA into your eQRP.

Example 1 - Owner of Wellness Chiropractic Corporation under age 50

Peter is 30 and the president and sole shareholder of Wellness Chiropractic Corporation, (a C Corporation) with 3 part time employees. Peter receives $250,000 in compensation from the corporation. In 2022 the maximum contribution Peter can make to his eQRP account is $61,000. This is $20,500 from his elective employee contribution and $40,500 from his employer profit sharing portion. The $40,500 employer contribution is the maximum allowed, (even though 25% of his taxable wages would be $62,500, the most he can receive from his employer is $40,500 per year).

Three of his part time employees have been with him for a few years are therefore required to receive non-elective deferrals. This means these three employees will receive 3% of their gross wages deducted and placed in their account as a non-elective deferral. This is not optional. The three employees' salaries are $30,000 per year each so the non-elective deferral is $900 per year.

Peter's profit-sharing employer contribution is a 2.5 to 1 match, meaning every dollar an employee contributes, the employer will contribute $2.5. He set this up so he can get the full $61,000 into his account. He contributes $20,500 and the employer contributes $2.5 for each dollar he contributes up to the max, $40,500.

The employees will get a matching profit-sharing contribution of $2.5 for each dollar they contribute. If they don't contribute, they would not receive any matching.

The Safe Harbor Plan rules are very complex and like all plans, any Safe Harbor plan should be thoroughly discussed with your tax advisor to verify current rules and nuances.

The theoretical net result is this:

	Employee Contribution Contribution	Employer Profit Sharing Contribution
Peter	$20,500	$40,500
Sam FTE #1	$900	$0
Sue FTE #2	$900	$0
Sally FTE #3	$900	$0

Sam, Sue and Sally can all contribute up to $20,500 of their income if they chose and Peter would have to contribute $2.5 for every $1, they contributed. One option he has to prevent this is to change the matching portion to zero. This would take away the threat of having all his employees contribute all their wages and cause a huge amount of employer required matching funds.

Minimum Vesting - Peter sets up a vesting schedule with a 3-year cliff. This means the employees matching portion is fully vested at the end of 3 years. If the employee was terminated, they'd get to take all the vested employer matching money with them. He also has the option of setting up a graduated vesting schedule. An example would be 20% a year for 5 years, so at the end of 2 years in service 20% of the matching funds would be vested, at the end of 3 years in service 40% would be vested etc. until all the money is vested at the end of 6 years. The first year in service he's not eligible for participation (unless the employer offers immediate enrollment).

Graduated Vesting

Years of Service	Non-forfeitable Percentage
2	0%
3	40%
4	60%
5	80%
6	100%

Cliff Vesting
Less than 3 years of service - 0% Vested
At least 3 years of service - 100% Vested

ROTH option

William decides he'd like to have a ROTH account for as much of his money as possible, so he takes his $20,500 employee elective deferral and puts it into a separate account labeled ROTH. This is after tax money, so he has to pay income taxes on this money the year he makes it. He is not allowed to have the Employer contribution/Profit Sharing identified as ROTH after tax funds, only his employee contribution.

Married

If William marries his girlfriend Wilma and she starts earning wages from the company she can contribute up to $20,500 from her earnings and 25% of her wages can be contributed from the employer profit sharing plan, so together they'd be able to contribute $100,000.

The Loan -

With an eQRP you're permitted to borrow money from your plan for any purpose at any time. Pursuant to Internal Revenue Code Section 72(p), the eQRP loan is permitted at any time using the accumulated balance of the eQRP as collateral for the loan. An eQRP participant can borrow up to either $50,000 or 50% of their account value-whichever is less. The loan must be repaid within 5 years and fully amortized within the chosen period of time with equal payments, no less then quarterly. The IRS requires a reasonable interest rate, which generally means prime plus 1%. Prime in 2021 was around 3% so a minimum safe rate would be around 4%. Of course, if you paid a higher amount this would be one legal strategy to get more money into your plan in addition to the annual contributions.

Internal Revenue Code Section 72(p) and the 2001 EGTRRA law established the framework for an eQRP participant to borrow money from his eQRP account. As long as the plan documents allow for it and the proper loan documents are prepared and executed, a participant can borrow money for his or her eQRP account for any purpose. The eQRP loan is received tax-free and penalty-free. There are no penalties or taxes due provided the loan payments are paid on time. The eQRP documents you receive from the eQRP Company allow you to borrow money from your eQRP for any purpose, including real estate, funding your own business, paying off personal debt, going on vacation etc.

The Ultimate Emergency Fund

Ever since the meltdown in 2008 banks have become more and more rigid about lending and have almost completely cut off lending to small businesses. The eQRP is a perfect structure for any self-employed business owner seeking immediate funds for their business without having to beg the bank

Investment Options

An eQRP plan allows you to invest in almost any type of investment you can think of other then the small list of disallowed items and disqualified persons. Any income and gains from an investment are required to go directly back to your eQRP plan and flow back tax free.

Some of the options you may choose to invest in are:

- ❑ Gold and Silver Bars and coins
- ❑ Real Estate, domestic and international
- ❑ Bitcoin
- ❑ Land
- ❑ Commercial paper, including mortgages
- ❑ Private businesses
- ❑ Stocks, Bonds and Mutual funds
- ❑ Foreign Currencies
- ❑ Private placements
- ❑ Tax liens

Disallowed Investments and Disqualified Persons

The Internal Revenue Code does not describe what an eQRP can invest in, only what it cannot invest in. Internal Revenue Code Section 4975 prohibits Disqualified Persons from engaging in certain type of transactions. The purpose of these rules is to encourage the use of retirement funds for accumulation and prohibit those in control of retirement funds from taking advantage of the tax benefits for their personal account. For a full list of disallowed items and the definition of a Disqualified Person, the disqualified information in Dirty.

EGTRRA - Clarifying the eQRP for a self-employed person

In 2001, the Economic Growth and Tax Relief Reconciliation Act (EGTRRA) was passed. This act clarified how a 401k or eQRP could be used by a self-employed person who has no full-time employees. It also clarified that the self-employed eQRP participant can make contributions as the role of employee and as employer. This dual contribution results in very high contribution limits.

Summary

The eQRP is a highly flexible and tax-efficient retirement solution that will allow you to make high contributions to the plan either pre-tax or by designating it a ROTH and building part of it 100% tax free.

- ❑ Contribute up to $61,000 a year ($67,500 if you're over 50)
- ❑ Borrow up to $50,000 or 50% of your account value (whichever is less)
- ❑ Invest in almost any type of investment tax free including:
- ❑ Precious metals like Gold, Silver and Platinum
- ❑ Real estate
- ❑ Tax liens

- ❑ Private businesses
- ❑ Private loans
- ❑ Main street stuff like stocks and bonds

With the eQRP you're able to use your retirement funds to make almost any type of investment on your own without requiring the "consent" of anyone else like a custodian. The last thing you want is some technical bureaucrat telling you what you can or can't do with your own money, especially when the IRS has been very specific about what the rules are. Why would you limit your choices by working with a custodian? Plus, you have to pay fees to this person for the service of telling you no!!!

As a trustee of your eQRP, you will have "Checkbook Control" over the eQRP assets.

The eQRP allows you to invest tax free in an investment that you know and understand and even allows you to borrow up to $50,000 or 50% of the account for any purpose.

Aside from certain "prohibited transactions" involving Disqualified Persons, which are outlined in the Internal Revenue Code Section 4975, an eQRP can invest in most of the commonly made investments, including real estate, private business entities, public and private shares in companies and commercial and private paper.

Self-employed individuals: You can make contributions on behalf of yourself only if you have net earnings (Compensation) from self-employment in the trade or business for which the plan was set up. Your net earnings must be from your personal services, not from your investments. If you have a net loss from self-employment, you cannot make contributions for yourself for the year, even if you can contribute for common-law employees based on their compensation.

What if you have a job that offers a 401k or other retirement plan?

You can participate in an employer's 401k plan in tandem with your own eQRP. In that case the employee-elective deferrals from both plans are subject to the single contribution limit. $20,500 in 2022 or $27,000 if over age 50

Employee Exemptions

The following types of employees may generally be excluded from coverage:

☐ Employees under 21 years of age
☐ Employees that work less than 1000 hours annually
☐ Union Employees
☐ Nonresident alien employees
☐ Employees that have worked for you less than a year.

Honey Badger Action Plan:

1. Set up the eQRP with the eQRP team. In 3 business days you'll receive your trust docs.
2. Provide your employees the eQRP disclosures
3. Rollover funds and assets. The eQRP company will guide your current custodian or trustee through the transfer process for any funds from old 401k, 403b or 457 plans. This is tax free and penalty free.
4. Contribute via Payroll. Start contributing as much as you can directly from your paycheck. Any contributions must be direct withdrawals from wages or earnings and transferred from your business account to the eQRP account. You are not permitted to deposit personal funds into your Safe Harbor eQRP 401k account. You will contribute any minimal or directed funds on behalf of employees through their non-elective and elective deferrals.

5. Invest. Invest in whatever you'd like - as long as you're investing in an allowed investment and not something disqualified or with a disqualified person you can write the check for the investment.

6. Management: Keep up with the bookkeeping on anything your eQRP does. The IRS requires basic record keeping. You can also hire a bookkeeper, accountant or third party to do this very inexpensively.

Section 6

The eQRP Dictionary

#

401 (k): A qualified retirement savings plan that allows employees to set aside tax- deferred income for retirement. In 2022, an employee can contribute up to $20,500 annually if they're under 50 or $27,000 if they're age 50 or over. A 401k is truly self-directed, allowing participants to invest in both traditional and non-traditional assets. Companies have the option to make matching contributions. This is a defined contribution plan. There are various 401k options: Roth, Traditional, Self- directed, and Profit-Sharing options.

A

Active Income: Income you are earning through actions performed for a company. This is any income based on employment and subject to social security and other taxes.

Annual Additions: The total of all an employee's contributions for a year. This does not include roll- over money from other accounts or previous years

Annual Benefits: What the employee receives yearly on an annuity basis. The benefits are the money taken out of the account (distribution), and they are taken on once every year.

Annuity: A specific amount of money received for a specific amount of time. For Example: Johnny gets $50,000/ year for 25 years. If Johnny dies the payments stop. There is no getting more or less money out, and usually there is no transferring the benefit. The amount received is the annual benefit.

B

Beneficiary: Person who receives the funds from the retirement plan. Just as the "benefit" is the money taken out, the beneficiary is the person who receives the money.

Business: A business is an activity in which a profit motive is present and economic activity is involved. Required to set up an eQRP.

C

Catch-up contribution: Additional employee contributions that can be made only by those who attain age 50 by the end of the year. This is what allows participants over 50 years old to add more into their retirement plans . . . so they can "catch up" to what a younger person would be able to contribute.

Cliff Vesting: This is when an employee is 100% vested on a given date. That date is the cliff that the employee has reached. For Example, a company says that an employee has full access to all the money that the company has put into their account (vested) when the employee has worked there for 2 years. In this example, the employee has no access to the money that the company put into the retirement account, until they have worked for that company for 2 years.

Collectible Items (as defined by the IRS): These are the items that are not allowed to be purchased with a retirement account:

- ❑ Any work of art,
- ❑ Any rug or antique,
- ❑ Any metal or gem,
- ❑ Any stamp or coin,

- • Acceptable Gold Coins (can be purchased with retirement accounts):

- ✓ A fifty-dollar gold coin that is 32.7 millimeters in diameter, weighs 33.931 grams, and contains one troy ounce of fine gold.
- ✓ A twenty-five-dollar gold coin that is 27.0 millimeters in diameter, weighs 16.966 grams, and contains one-half troy ounce of fine gold.
- ✓ A ten-dollar gold coin that is 22.0 millimeters in diameter, weighs 8.483 grams, and contains one-fourth troy ounce of fine gold.
- ✓ A five-dollar gold coin that is 16.5 millimeters in diameter, weighs 3.393 grams, and contains one-tenth troy ounce of fine gold.

- Acceptable Silver Coins (can be purchased with retirement accounts):

  - ✓ are 40.6 millimeters in diameter and weigh 31.103 grams.
  - ✓ contain .999 fine silver;
  - ✓ have a design—
  - ✓ symbolic of Liberty on the obverse side; and
  - ✓ of an eagle on the reverse side;
  - ✓ have inscriptions of the year of minting or issuance, and the words "Liberty," "In God We Trust," "United States of America," "1 Oz. Fine Silver," "E Pluribus Unum," and "One Dollar,"; and
  - ✓ have reeded edges.

Common Law Employee: Any person under common law would be considered an employee. For example, if the employer provides the employee's tools, materials, and workplace, and the employer can fire them person, they are a common- law employee. Common Law employees are not self- employed and cannot set up retirement plan for themselves.

Compensation: All the payments an employee receives, including wages and salaries, fees for professional services, commissions and tips, fringe benefits, and bonuses. Compensation also includes any elective deferrals. Compensation does not include nontaxable reimbursement, like expenses or non-elective deferrals.

Conduit IRA: An IRA that was funded with a rolled over 401k, or other qualified retirement plan, such as 403b or 457.

Contribution Deadline: The last moment someone can add money to their retirement plan that year. For a qualified plan, this can actually be after the tax return is completed, and the return can be used to fund the account for the same year. You can make deductible contributions for a tax year up to the due date of your return (plus extensions) for that year. You can make contributions on behalf of yourself only if you have net earnings (Compensation) from self-employment in the trade or business for which the plan was set up. Your net earnings must be from your personal services, not from your investments. If you have a net loss from self-employment, you cannot make contributions for yourself for the year, even if you can contribute for common-law employees based on their compensation.

You generally apply your plan contributions to the year in which you make them. But you can apply them to the previous year if all the following requirements are met.

- ❑ You make them by the due date of your tax return for the previous year (including extensions).
- ❑ The plan was established by the end of the previous year.
- ❑ The plan treats the contributions as though it had received them on the last day of the previous year.

Contribution Limits: The amount that an employee or employer can no longer receive tax benefits for. So, you can put as much money as you want into a retirement account, but after a certain dollar amount, you no longer receive the tax benefits from those contributions. There is no penalty for taking that extra money out of the account, if the contributor goes over the limit.

Coverage: Qualified plans must include a certain percentage of rank-and-file employees.

D

Deadline to Contribute - see Contribution deadline

Defined Benefit Plan: This is essentially a pension. This account has a set amount that the beneficiary will receive at retirement. Because the end result is set, contributions change based on how the account is performing. Not knowing how the investments will perform, means the employee, and the employer are less able to prepare and plan on their contributions, because the goal is set, not the contribution. These are great for CEO's and those who want to contribute significantly more money to their retirement.

Defined Contribution Plan: These are individual plans, and the outcome, the result, the amount you get at retirement is based on how much the employee puts in (contributes) and how the investments perform. So, this means the plan is defined, or run by the contributions that are put into the accounts. These are the IRA's, 401k's, profit sharing plans, etc. So, there are some Defined Contribution Plans that are Qualified Retirement Plans, and some that are Unqualified.

Disqualified Persons: The IRS has determined that there are some people the participant is not allowed to purchase things from when using their qualified retirement plan. Congress did this to prevent certain parties from doing suspicious or fraudulent deals. See FAQ's under Disqualified Persons

Disallowed Investments: A few things that a qualified retirement plan cannot be used to purchase or fund.

E

Early Distribution: Anytime you take money out of your retirement plan before age 59.5 is early. For most early distributions the participant must pay a 10% penalty, plus the tax penalty (which is at the rate of income tax) for the distribution. There are a few exceptions that allow you to bypass the 10% penalties, but the participant will still pay the income tax. If the participant dies, their beneficiary has immediate access to their account. If the participant is disabled, there is no penalty for the early distribution. If the participant sets it up as annuity for the rest of their life expectancy, then there is no 10% penalty (this helps the government, they are guaranteed monthly tax distribution, so they allow it). A few other exemptions are: if you leave your company after age 55; you need it to pay your child support; if you put more into the account than you are allowed to deduct from your taxes, you can take out the excess; medical expenses; or mandatory distributions (you are 72 years old, but not retired).

Earned Income: Net earnings from self-employment, from a business that you directly impacted with your work. This would also include any royalties from a book or invention. Earnings from personal effort or labor are subject to self-employment tax, including social security tax.

Elective Deferral: The amount of pre-tax salary that the employee chooses to put into a retirement plan. This only applies to accounts that use pre-tax dollars, like the 401k. A Roth 401k would use after tax dollars.

Your qualified plan can include a cash or deferred arrangement under which participants can choose to have you contribute part of their before – tax compensation to the plan rather than receive the compensation in cash. A plan with this type of arrangement is popularly known as a "401k plan." (As a self-employed individual participating in the plan, you can contribute part of your before-tax net earnings from the business). This contribution is called an "elective" deferral" because participants choose (elect) to defer receipt of the money. In general, a qualified plan can include a cash or deferred arrangement only if the qualified plan is one of the following:

❑ A Profit sharing plan
❑ Matching contributions. If your plan permits you can make matching contributions for an employee who makes an elective deferral to your 401k plan. For example, the plan might provide that you will contribute 50 cents for each dollar your participating employees choose to defer under your 401k plan.

Eligible Rollover Distribution: Often, an eligible rollover distribution occurs when an individual leaves the service of an employer. The rollover rules allow the individual to bring the assets to their IRAs or a retirement plan at a new employer.

Read more:

http://www.investopedia.com/terms/e/
eligiblerolloverdistribution.asp#ixzz2AKv6c3Xm

Enrollment Period: The time frame that someone can sign up for a qualified retirement plan.

EGTRRA (Economic Growth and Tax Relief Reconciliation Act): Law put into place in 2001 to allow for a higher rate of annual contributions for employees, and employers using profit sharing, as well as make the accounts easier to access. Among some of the changes is that this law added the "catch up" provision. Small employers are granted tax incentives to offer retirement plans to their employees, and sole proprietors, partners, and S corporation shareholders gain the right to take loans from their company pension plans.

http://www.nysscpa.org/reconciliationact/reconciliationact1.htm

Elective deferrals: The portion of an employee's salary that is contributed to a retirement plan. This could be on a pretax basis or, if the plan allows a Roth option, a post tax basis. Elective deferrals apply in the case of 401k plans, 403(b) annuities, SARSEPs (established before 1997), and SIMPLE plans.

ERISA: Employee Retirement Income Security Act of 1974 is a federal law that establishes minimum standards for pension plans in private industry. ERISA was enacted to protect the interests of employee benefit plan participants and their beneficiaries by requiring the financial, and other, information concerning the plan to beneficiaries. The act also established standards of conduct for plan fiduciaries. And gives the participants of these plans access to the federal courts.

Employer: An employer is any person for whom an individual performs or has performed any service, of whatever nature, as an employee. A sole proprietor is treated as his or her own employer for retirement plan purposes. In a partnership, the partnership is treated as the employer of each partner for retirement plan purposes.

Excess contribution penalty: A six-percent cumulative penalty imposed on an employer for making contributions in excess of contribution limits.

F

Fiduciary: A legal relationship of trust. A person who exercises any discretionary authority or control over the management of the plan or its assets, or who is paid to give investment advice regarding plan assets. Plan service providers such as actuaries, attorneys, accountants, brokers, and record keepers are NOT fiduciaries unless they exercise discretion or are responsible for the management of the plan or its assets.

Every plan document must clearly identify one or more persons to be the named fiduciary for the plan. If there is only one named fiduciary, that person or entity will be considered a fiduciary for all purposes under the plan. If there is more than one named fiduciary, the named fiduciaries can allocate responsibilities among themselves. The purpose of the named fiduciary designation is to clearly identify to participants and government agencies who is primarily responsible for the plan.

Fiduciaries have important responsibilities and are subject to standards of conduct because they act on behalf of participants in a retirement plan and their beneficiaries. These responsibilities include:

❑ Acting solely in the interest of plan participants and their beneficiaries and with the exclusive purpose of providing benefits to them;
❑ Carrying out their duties prudently;
❑ Following the plan documents (unless inconsistent with ERISA);
❑ Diversifying plan investments; and
❑ Paying only reasonable plan expenses.

Funding: In the case of defined benefit plans, the amount of assets required to be in the plan in order to meet plan liabilities (current and future pension obligations).

H

Hardship Withdrawal: Taking money out of a qualified retirement plan without penalty, when certain requirements are met. Not all plans allow hardship withdrawals; this has to be allowed by the employer. The employee can only withdrawal their own contributions, the employer contributions cannot be taken out for a hardship withdrawal. The requirements for a hardship withdrawal are as follows: It must satisfy an immediate and financial need of the employee, such as: medical expenses, the purchase of a primary residence, payment of tuition or other educational needs, payment necessary to prevent eviction.

Highly Compensated Employee: An employee who owned more than 5% of the interest in a business at any time during the year or the preceding year, regardless on compensation. This can also be defined as someone who received $115,000 in the preceding year. It is also possible to define a Highly Compensated Employee as an employee who is in the top 20% in the compensation bracket at the company.

I

In-service Distributions: This is another way to get at the money before retirement. The law will allow you to take distributions in very limited circumstances from your profit-sharing plan while your business is still in operation. Those circumstances are: after participant has been on the plan for a fixed number of years (usually at least 2); after the participant reaches a certain age (which is determined by the plan); if there is an extraneous circumstance, such as a layoff, illness, disability, retirement, death or termination of employment. An in-service distribution that is moved directly into another qualified plan is considered a rollover and does not trigger a taxable event.

IRA: Retirement plan that any individual can open without the assistance of a company. Hence the term Individual Retirement Account. IRA was originally created for those that are not covered by a qualified plan. There are now 5 variations on IRA plans. All IRA plans have hefty restrictions on contribution limits and how the account can be funded.

K

Key Employee: This could be the same as a highly compensated employee in some small businesses. Someone that has a large stake in the company, an owner or partner in the company. A key employee during 2022 is generally an employee who is either of the following.

- ❑ An officer having annual pay of more than $200,000.
- ❑ An employee who is either of the following.

  - A 5% owner of your business.
  - A 1% owner of your business whose annual pay was more than $150,000.

L

Loan: A person can take out a loan from their retirement plan without penalty, if they repay it within 5 years with fixed payments and using a reasonable amount of interest. They can borrow up to $50,000 or 50% of the assets, whichever is less, and if they qualify based on length the account has been open, person's age, and /or a hardship situation.

Leased employee: A person is considered a leased employee if they provide services to an employer according to an agreement between the employer and the leasing organization, provides services on a substantially full-time basis, and provides services under the control of the employer. For retirement plan purposes, a leased employee who is not your common-law employee must generally be treated as your employee.

M

Mandatory Minimum Distributions: Once the employee or beneficiary reaches retirement or age 72, they must take out money from their account. It is required by law and mandatory, there is a "lowest amount" = Minimum, taken from an account and given to the account owner= Distribution.

If the account balance of a qualified plan participant is to be distributed (other than as an annuity), the plan administrator must figure the minimum amount required to be distributed each distribution calendar year. This minimum is figured by dividing the account balance by the applicable life expectancy. A participant must begin to receive distributions from his or her qualified retirement plan by April 1 of the first year after the later of the following years.

- ❑ Calendar year in which he or she reaches age 72
- ❑ Calendar in which he or she retires from employment with the employer maintaining the plan.

However, the plan may require the participant to begin receiving distributions by April 1 of the year after the participant reaches age 72 even if the participant has not retired.

Master and prototype plans: Plans typically designed by companies to be used for qualified retirement plans that comply with IRS plan requirements.

Match: What the company contributes into the retirement plan to encourage the employee to contribute. This is an amount based on what the employee contributes. There are limits to how much the employer can contribute, with the maximum being 40,500 per year per employee in 2022. The amount matched can be up to 20% of the employees' wages in a sole proprietorship, partnership or LLC and 25% of the wages in a corporation.

Mega Back Door Roth: The secret plan the rich use to super contribute money into a roth account. Current law allows the eQRP owner to contribute $61,000 into Roth each year with earnings of less than $70,000. This means you can generally contribute 100% of your earnings into a Roth account. Book a strategy call with eQRP to learn more: eqrp.co/strategy

Money Purchase Pension Plan: A simple plan that allows employers to easily plan for their expenses, because it is a set amount that they contribute. This also gives employees a sense of stability and comfort, because they know what is going to be contributed. This method does not connect the employee's performance with their contribution, so may not provide the incentive that they employer would like.

N

Net earnings from self-employment: Net earnings from self-employment for SEP and qualified plans is your gross income from your trade or business (provided your personal services are a material income-producing factor) minus allowable business deductions.

For the deduction limits, earned income is net earnings for personal services actually rendered to the business. When calculating net earnings, you take into account the income tax deduction for one-half of self-employment tax and the deduction for contributions to the plan made on your behalf. The deduction for self-employment heath insurance is disregarded when figuring the deduction for one-half of self-employment tax.

Net earnings include a partner's distributive share of partnership income or loss (other than separately stated items, such as capital gains and losses). Guaranteed payments to limited partners are net earnings from self-employment as long as they are paid for services to or for the partnership. Distributions of other income or loss to limited partners and income passed through to shareholders of S Corporations are not considered net earnings from self-employment.

Nondiscrimination: Requirements to provide benefits for rank-and-file employees and not simply to favor owners and highly paid employees.

Non-elective deferral: The amount the company contributes to the Safe Harbor 401k plan. This is an amount that the company promises to contribute to the employee's account that is not based on a percentage of what the employee contributes.

Non-traditional investment: Investing in something outside of the normal realm of finances. This would include, but is not limited to: Real Estate, Coins (gold, silver, and platinum), Intellectual and Digital property, Art and Antiques.

Non-Qualified Retirement Plan: These are retirement funds that do not follow the guidelines and rules Congress has passed into law and thus cannot take advantage of most of the benefits a qualified plan.

Non-recourse loans: The only type of loans allowed for a retirement plan. According to rules and regulations, the holder of the account, the Self-Directed IRA plan, or any business entity funded by the plan cannot be held liable for the loan repayment.

P

Participant: Any eligible employee who is covered by your retirement plan

Partner: One who shares ownership of an unincorporated trade of business with one or more persons.

Passive Income: Anything earned through an investment, such as interest or dividends earned on stocks, bonds, or savings. Something earned just buy owning something. . . no duties or actions were performed.

PBGC: The Pension Benefit Guaranty Corporation is an independent agency of the US government that was created by the ERISA to encourage the encourage the continued use of voluntary private benefit pension plans, provide timely and uninterrupted payment to pension benefits, and keep pension insurance premiums at the lowest level possible and still stay functioning. The annuity guaranteed is set. There is also an option to take out all the money in one lump sum, which is also a set amount.

Pension Protection Act: This act allows a person to make an additional 6% profit sharing contribution (up to maximum $250,000 in 2022) and may contribute $20,500 pretax into a separate 401k plan in 2022. This is a way to save more for retirement. The profit sharing does not count toward the 401k limit.

Plan Administrator: A plan administrator is responsible for determining who is eligible to participate in the plan, determining what benefits are due under the plan, and responding to benefit claims and appeals. Plan administrators also have responsibilities dictated under the Internal Revenue Code (Code) and Employment Retirement Income Security Act of 1974 (ERISA) as follows:

- ❏ Distribution of summary plan description, summary annual reports, and statement of vested benefits to participants and beneficiaries
- ❏ For plans with over 100 participants, engaging an independent qualified public accountant to audit the financial records of the plan
- ❏ Maintenance of plan records for at least six years
- ❏ Determination of whether a domestic relations order is qualified and
- ❏ Providing a written explanation of rollover and tax withholding election options, as well as an explanation of tax options with respect to distributions to recipients.

Profit Sharing Plan: A defined contribution plan where the company agrees to make substantial and recurring contributions. The contributions are flexible and usually based on the existence of profits.

Prohibited Transactions: There are some limits on what you can do with your retirement plan. Basically, it can't be used as a tool to only benefit the company. It cannot be a vehicle to benefit the fiduciary or plan administrator. There is a list in Code Section 4975

Q

Qualified Domestic Relations Order (QDRO): This gives divorcing couples a vehicle to protect plan assets and minimize tax and penalties. This anti-alienation usually keeps the qualified retirement plan safe from anyone else, but in the case of divorce, the participant is able to transfer the funds to someone else (such as the soon to be former spouse).

Qualified Employee: An employee that is able to participate in a qualified retirement plan. The rules to participate must be equal for all employees and include all employees of a particular category. If you want to provide the plan to part time employees, who work

10+ hours a week on average, then you must provide it to ALL employees who work an average of 10 hours a week or more. This program cannot be provided based on performance.

Qualified Retirement Plan: Retirement plans that offer a tax favored way to save for retirement. Qualified Retirement Plans include the eQRP, 401k's, Profit Sharing Plans, Money Purchases Plans, and Defined Benefit Plans. These plans were designed by the government to encourage companies to help their employees save for retirement by giving both the employee and the employer tax incentives. All Qualified Retirement Plans are regulated by ERISA and the Department of Labor and have requirements that each plan must meet to be considered a qualified retirement plan. A plan must offer life annuities, maintain a sufficient level of funds, administered according to the plan document, must require funds withdrawn at retirement (or age 72, whichever comes first), the plan cannot favor highly compensated employees, and must be insured by the Pension Benefit Guaranty Corporation (PBGC).

Qualified Distributions: A qualified distribution is a distribution that is made after the employee's non-exclusion period and:

- ❑ On or after the employee attains age 59 ½
- ❑ On account of the employee's being disabled, or
- ❑ On or after the employees' death

The eQRP: The Ferrari of 401k retirement plans

R

Rank and File Employee: The non-executive and non-managerial employees of a company.

Reporting Requirements: Any plan with assets of $250,000 or more is required to file a form 5500 with the IRS by the last day of the

7ᵗʰ month after the plan year ends. Any plan that has less than 100 employees and less than $250,000 in assets is exempt from filing.

Required minimum distributions: Plans must begin to distribute benefits to employees at a certain time. Generally, benefits must begin to be paid out no later that April 1 following the year in which a participant attains age 72. Failure to receive required minimum distributions results in a 50% tax on the amount not withdrawn.

Rollover: A tax free and penalty free transfer of funds and assets from one qualified plan to another on behalf of the owner. Typically, this takes place when someone leaves the employment of a company or government and had built up a 401k or another type of qualified account. There are requirements to roll money from one account to another. Usually, the account owner must transfer the money from one like account to another (from traditional to traditional or Roth to Roth) to prevent any penalties or taxes being charged. Rollovers can require 20% of the account withheld if the rollover funds are distributed to the owner first and do not go directly to a new trustee.

Roth 401k: A retirement plan that takes after tax contributions. The distributions and the fund fluctuations (interest rates, dividends, losses, etc.) are all untaxed.

Roth IRA: A non-qualified retirement plan whose contributions are post tax. Original contributions can be withdrawn at any point without tax or penalty regardless of owner's age. Distributions that include earnings are tax free, so long as the owner is at least 59 1/2 years old.

S

Safe Harbor™ eQRP 401k: This is a type of 401k plan that requires everyone to be 100% vested from the beginning. This plan also requires certain minimum benefits to eligible employees either in the form of matching or non-elective contributions. This also allows for more design flexibility and allows the employee to take out funds for loans or hardship withdrawal. See the Honey Badger chapter

Self- Employed Individual: Someone in business for him or herself, and whose business is not incorporated. Self-employed can include part-time work and include sole proprietors and partners.

Self-Employed Qualified Plans: The plans that people who work for themselves can open. The self-employed person can have elective deferrals and employer contributions

Slide Vesting: This is an option to vest an employee a little at a time. This means the employee has access to the money the employer (company) has put into the retirement account a certain percent each year. For Example: Say an employee starts with Company XYZ, which offers a sliding vesting of 20% a year. That means that each year the employee works for Company XYZ, they have access to 20% more of the money that Company XYZ put into the retirement account. If the employee stays at Company XYZ for 3 years, then employee can take 60% of Company XYZ's deposits (or contributions) into that account, the rest goes back to the company.

Salary reduction arrangements: Arrangements to make contributions to qualified plans from an employee's compensation on a pretax basis. In general, salary reduction arrangements relate to 401k plans, 403(b) annuities, SARSEPs in existence before 1997, and SIMPLE plans.

Savings incentive match plans of employees (SIMPLE): IRA-or 401k type plans that permit modest employee contributions via salary reduction and require modest employer contributions.

Simplified employee pensions (SEP): IRAs set up by employees to which an employer makes contributions based on a percentage of income.

Sole proprietor: A sole proprietor is an individual who owns an unincorporated business by him/herself. This includes a single member limited liability company (owned by one individual) that is treated as a disregarded entity for tax purposes. A sole proprietor is treated as both an employer and an employee for retirement plan purposes.

Stock bonus plan: Defined contribution plans that give participants shares of stock in the employer rather than cash.

Summary Annual Report (SAR): This document describes the financial information in the plan's Annual REport, the Form 5500, and is provided on an annual basis to participants in a narrative form.

Summary Plan Description (SPD): This basic descriptive document is a plain language explanation and must be comprehensive enough to apprise participants of their rights and responsibilities under the plan It also tells participants of the plan features and what to expect from the plan. For Example an SPD must include:

- ❑ When and how employees become eligible to participate;
- ❑ The source of contributions and contribution levels;
- ❑ The vesting period, i.e., the length of time an employee must belong to a plan to receive benefits from it;
- ❑ How to file a claim for those benefits; and
- ❑ A participant's basic rights and responsibilities under ERISA.

This document is given to employees after they join the plan and to beneficiaries after they first receive benefits. SPDs must also be redistributed periodically and provided on request

Summary of Material Modification (SMM): This document tells participants and beneficiaries of changes to the plan or to the information required to be in the SPD. The SMM or an updated SPD for a retirement plan must be provided to participants within 210 days after the end of the plan year in which the change was put into place.

T

Taxable Income: This is the amount that the IRS uses to determine what you will pay in income taxes. So, this is the amount before deductions, before tax deferred contributions, and the amount before taxes are taken out.

Tax-deferred: Current income that is taxed at a later date usually by putting it into an eQRP or other retirement plan

Top-heavy plans: Qualified retirement plans that provide more than a certain amount of benefits or contributions to owners and/ or highly paid employees. Top-heavy plans have special vesting schedules.

TPA (Third Party Administrator): This party, person or company keeps records etc.

Trustee: The person who accepts funds, manages them prudently and distributes them to the beneficiaries. A plan sponsor can either choose individual trustees - usually the owners or officers of the business - or a single institutional trustee, such as an affiliate of a bank, insurance company or other financial institution.

All plan assets must be held in a trust, and a plan trustee must be named. The trustee holds plan assets and is usually responsible for managing the plan's investments, although this function can be subject to the direction of another fiduciary, an investment manager, or plan participants. The plan trustee is usually responsible for processing contributions and investment transactions, preparing financial statements, and disbursing funds to participants or to pay fees and expenses of the trust.

U

UBIT (Unrelated Business Income Tax): the tax on unrelated business income, which comes from an activity engaged in by a tax-exempt 26 USCA 501 organization that is not related to the tax-exempt purpose of that organization. For most organizations, a business activity generates unrelated business income subject to taxation if it fails to sufficiently relate to the tax-exempt purpose of that tax exempt organization if it meets three requirements:

1. It is a trade or business,
2. It is regularly carried on, and
3. It is not substantially related to furthering the exempt purpose of the organization

§408(e)(1) states: "Any individual retirement account is exempt from taxation under this subtitle unless such account has ceased to be an individual retirement account. In addition, the IRS unequivocally confirms this in the first few paragraphs of Chapter 1 of the November 2007 revision of Publication 598 that IRAs are "subject to the tax on unrelated business income."

UDFI (Unrelated Debt-Financed Income): Income generated by an IRA or other retirement plan like the eQRP through debt financing or leverage. UDFI only applies to the profit realized through debt and is based on the highest amount of leverage carried within the past 12 months.

❏ **The eQRP is EXEMPT from UDFI. An IRA is not exempt and is subject to paying the UDFI penalty tax.**

An example would be if your self-directed IRA purchased a rental home in 2015 for $200,000 using a non-recourse loan with 30% down. Your IRA has secured a 70% loan to value (LTV) on the rental home. To make it easy let's assume you never paid down the principal. In 2022, you sold that same piece of property for $400,000. 70% of the profit would be subject to UBIT because it was generated by money that was not related to the self-directed IRA. Keep in mind the 70% subject to the tax would be subject to depreciation and write offs just like with a standard mortgage. This tax is currently 37% max, brutal!

Note: If the self-directed IRA can pay off its loan early, it may not have to pay UBIT at all. UDFI does not apply if debt is paid off 12 months prior to the sale of the property.

If you used your eQRP instead of the IRA, you would not be subject to UDFI

V

Vested: Indicates how much of the employer contributed money in the retirement plan that the employee gets to take with them, if they leave the company. There are some instances when the employee (worker) is 100% vested on day X. This would mean, the employee can take all the money that the employer (company) put into the account, once the employee has worked for that employer for X days. There is also an option to have the employee receive a percent of the money each year. For Example: For simplicity sake, let's say you make $30,000. If your employer contributes 6% of your annual income each year, they add $1800/ year. If you decide to leave that company after 3 years, you may not get the entire $5400 that the company put into the account. You have to know how much you are "vested" each year . . . what percent of that money you get to take with you. Let's say you get 20% more vested each year. When you decide to leave after 3 years, you are

60% vested. In other words, you get to keep 60% of the money that they company contributed. In this example, you would get to keep $3240 (plus whatever amount you contributed from your paycheck, that money is always yours). See also Cliff Vesting and Slide Vesting for more information and Honey Badger Chapter for more examples.

X

Xanadu: Where you will retire

Y

You: The person reading this book (also see brilliant, and on your way).

Z

Zealous: How you will feel once you have opened your eQRP account! Ardent, enthusiastic about what a good decision this retirement plan is, eager to see your genius in play, earnest

CASE STUDY

Reduce Corporate Taxes and Minimize Personal Income Taxes

ABC Personal Corporation, Inc.

Net Income	$100,000
2022 Federal and State tax rate of 40%	$40,000

OBJECTIVE:

How to reduce corporation taxes and minimize personal income taxes?

ANSWER:

Employer contributes 25% of W-2 to Profit Sharing Plan and employee makes maximum elective deferral to the 401k plan.

John & Mary Jones – 100% Stockholders

		Bonus	Total Comp
John's current salary	$30,000	$20,000	$ 50,000
Mary's current salary	$30,000	$20,000	$ 50,000
	$52,000	$40,000	$100,000

STEP 1: John and Mary elect to defer the maximum of their bonus to the eQRP 401k plan by making an elective deferral (both are over 50 years of age) of $27,000 each

RESULT: $20,000 bonus – elective deferral of $27,000 = $4,000 taxable on their personal tax return. Reduction in personal income on their Form 1040 of $54,000 ($27,000 x 2)

STEP 2: Corporation contributes the max (25%) of their W-2 wages (in excess of their elective deferrals) ($11,125) to the Profit Sharing Plan and Corporation takes a deduction for this amount.

RESULT: Corporation deducts $11,125 on its tax return – no payroll on income taxes on this amount.

New tax results for corporation and individual are as follows:

Corporation

Taxable income	$100,000
Less bonuses	- 40,000
Profit Sharing Contribution	- 11,125
Taxable Income	$ 48,875
Taxable rate 40%	.40
$ 19,550	
Reduction in taxes	$20,450

Personal Income Tax Return

Personal income increased by $20,000 each	$40,000
Taxable rate 30%	.30
Tax Increase	$12,000

Income Tax Summary of Results

Corporate Tax Decrease	$ 20,450
Personal Tax Increase	+ 12,000
Net Income Tax Decrease	$ 8,450

Payroll Tax Decrease on
Profit Sharing Contribution
15.3% x 11,125 $ 1,702

Total Tax Savings $ 10,152

SAFE HARBOR eQRP 401k PLAN

SAFE HARBOR eQRP 401k PLAN FEATURES

❑ Allows all participants to contribute up to maximum annual deferral limit ($20,500 in 2022), plus "catch up" ($6500) contributions for employees age 50 and over.
❑ Requires a flat contribution of 3% of pay or a 100% match on salary deferrals up to 4% of pay
❑ Eliminates the burden of restrictive discrimination testing.
❑ Allocation of additional profit sharing may be customized to benefit plan sponsors and/or select groups of employees.
❑ Vesting of required contributions is 100% immediately.
❑ Allows additional matching and/or profit sharing contributions.

SAMPLE SAFE HARBOR eQRP 401k PLAN - 2022

Compensation		Salary Deferral	Profit Sharing	Total Contribution
Participant	$ 20,000	discretionary	$ 600	$ 600
Participant	$ 40,000	discretionary	$ 1,200	$ 1,200
Participant	$ 50,000	discretionary	$ 1,500	$ 1,500
Owner	$245,000	$27,000	$ 40,500	$ 67,500
Totals	$355,000	$27,000	$ 43,800	$ 70,800

ARTICLES

Inherited IRAs not protected in bankruptcy

By Renee Rodda, J.D.

The Bankruptcy Court has determined that, unlike a debtor's own traditional IRA, an inherited IRA is not an exempt asset of the bankruptcy Code §522 (d) (12).

The Court concluded that funds in an inherited IRA are not funds intended for retirement purposes but, instead, are distributed to the beneficiary of the account without regard to age or retirement status.

It is generally believed that IRAs are protected in a bankruptcy proceeding, unless the funds have been used in a prohibited transaction. **The decision in this case means that taxpayers with financial difficulties may lose any inherited IRAs in a bankruptcy proceeding.**

Excluded Accounts

The bankruptcy estate includes nearly all legal and equitable rights of the debtor, as well as those interests recovered or recoverable through transfer and lien avoidance provisions. However, certain assets are specifically excluded under the Bankruptcy Code and may not be used to pay creditors.

Bankruptcy Code §522(d)(12) excluded retirement funds to the extent that those funds are in a fund or account that is exempt from taxation under IRC §§401, 403, 408, 408A, 414, 457, or 501(a).

To determine whether an account is an "exempt" retirement account, the court must determine that:

❑ The funds are retirement funds; and
❑ That the funds are exempt from tax under the specified code sections.

Note: The maximum amount that can be protected in an IRA account during a bankruptcy proceeding is $1 million.

The Inherited Account

Although there is no dispute that the original IRA was a retirement account, which was exempt from taxation, the original owner's death and the distribution of the funds to her daughter transformed the nature of the IRA. Her daughter placed the distributed funds into a new IRA account created in her deceased mother's name from which she, as the beneficiary of the new account, must take distributions prior to retirement.

Even assuming that the inherited IRA contains "retirement funds," the account established by the beneficiary to receive the distribution of funds from her mother's IRA is not a traditional IRA exempt from taxation under IRC§408(e)(1). Although an inherited IRA is exempt from tax under IRC§402(c)(11), this is not one of the specific code sections listed in the bankruptcy code.

New Roth Conversion Law

On September 27, 2010, President Obama signed into law the "Small Business Jobs Act of 2010." This law contains a provision that allows 401k and 403(b) plans to permit participants to convert some or all of their existing pretax amounts into Roth accounts within the existing savings plan. This optional provision applies only if a savings plan allows participants to make Roth contributions. It eliminates the need for employees and spousal beneficiaries to roll non-Roth money out of their retirement plan and into a Roth IRA in order to take advantage of the Roth program.

The following types of plans are permitted to allow the Roth conversion: 401k Plans, 403(b) Plans, and governmental 457(b) Plans. This provision does not apply to money purchase pension plans, profit sharing plans, or defined benefit plans.

Listed below are some important facts about the Roth conversion feature:

- ❑ A Roth feature must be offered as part of the plan, in order for Roth conversions to be permitted within the plan.
- ❑ This conversation is only available to participants who have a distributable event, that would allow them to withdraw (termination, disability, death, attaining age 59½).
- ❑ This conversion applies to amounts treated as eligible rollover distributions; it disqualifies hardships, requires minimum distributions, and corrective distributions.

Section 7

FAQ's

1. What is a Qualified Retirement Plan?

The technical definition for a qualified plan is one that satisfies the requirements of IRC Section 401(a). A Qualified Plan is known for the numerous tax advantages the plan allows. Contributions made into the plan are not taxed until you withdraw the money, which allows an investor to save more money than in other types of retirement plans. A qualified plan is established by a business and is subject to the provisions of the Employee Retirement Income Security Act (ERISA). Some of the most common types of qualified retirement plans consist of Profit-Sharing Plans, 401k plans, eQRPs and Defined Benefit Plans

2. How many kinds of Qualified Retirement Plans are there?

There are two basic kinds of qualified plans: defined contribution plans and defined benefit plans-and different rules apply to each. You can have more than one qualified plan, but your contributions to all the plans must not total more than the overall limit.

3. Why Have a Qualified Retirement Plan?

❑ **Unlimited Options & Tax Deferral**

An eQRP offers a business owner the ability to use his retirement funds to make virtually any type of investment tax-free, including real estate, on his own without requiring the consent of a custodian. The IRS only describes the disqualified investments, and very few at that! All the income and gains goes back to your eQRP tax free!

❑ High Contribution Limits

An IRA allows you to contribute $6000 a year, or $7,000 if you're over age 50, to "catch up." The problem with this is that you can only get $100,000 into the plan over 20 years. That's just not enough to get close to what you'll need for retirement.

With an eQRP you can contribute $61,000 per person, up to $122,000 with a spouse and even more if you're over 50. ($67,500 each in 2022, if over 50 years old)

❑ Other Benefits

Qualified retirement plans can provide many tax and non-tax benefits to employers as well as to employees, such as:

- Help employers attract and retain better employees, thereby reducing turnover and new employee training costs.
- Employers can immediately deduct their contributions (within certain limits) into a qualified plan and may even be entitled to receive a tax credit for a part of the costs of implementing the plan. The balance of the cost can be deducted on your tax return.
- Employees pay no income tax on employer contributions (within certain limitations) until the funds are distributed.
- Employees benefit from the tax-free accumulation of earnings.
- Employees generally may make pretax contributions from their compensation to a qualified plan, called elective deferrals (thereby lowering participants' taxable income).

- One of the greatest advantages of qualified plans is that retirement savings from defined contribution plans are portable. Eligible funds can be rolled over to another defined contribution plan (or IRA), in accordance with certain requirements, thereby helping employees continue to build their retirement funds and cut down on the excess paperwork caused by maintaining several retirement accounts.

- The U.S. government will even pay you back a portion of your contribution to a retirement plan up to $1,000 each year per participant for taxpayers in low tax brackets. Form 8880 is used to claim the credit.

4. How are gains handled? Can you defer through 1031?

That's the cool thing, it's automatically ALL deferred because it's inside the plan. You never buy anything that you are getting a benefit from, that's considered a disqualified investment.

5. Do I need to have a business in order to set up a plan?

Yes, you will need to have a business in order to set up a plan. Your business is called the plan sponsor. You have a lot of flexibility to choose the type of business you'd like to have including a sole proprietorship, LLC, Partnership or Corporation. This is as simple as having an online store like an eBay store or mowing your neighbor's lawn.

6. Is there a minimum amount of income my business needs before I set up my plan?

There are no minimum income limits for an eQRP. You can only use your income from the business that the eQRP account is associated with, but you don't have to make a certain amount.

7. What happens if I have several different businesses? Can I still use all of my income to calculate my contribution to the plan?

If you own the majority control of all your businesses, you can establish one plan and have the other businesses adopt the plan. However, if you do not have majority ownership in all the businesses, you will want to set up separate plans for each. Separate. Having an eQRP plan for each business is also beneficial if you want to be more aggressive with specific investments or contributions for a certain business.

8. How do I get an eQRP? How long does it take?

Either visit eQRP.co or Call: 800-270-1649. The information required will take about 10 minutes to gather and then you'll receive your trust documents for your eQRP within 48 hours.

The Basic Steps in Setting UP an eQRP plan:

A) a Written Plan that describes the benefit structure and guides day-to-day operations
B) Federal ID#
C) either contribute tax deductible contributions on roll over funds other
D) retirement plan such as IRA, etc or elective deferrals.

You, the employer, are responsible for setting up and maintaining the plan. *TIP—If you are self-employed, it is not necessary to have employees besides yourself to sponsor and set up a qualified plan.*

SET-UP DEADLINE. To take a deduction for contributions for a tax year, your eQRP plan must be set up (adopted) by the time you file your tax return. Yes, this means you can do tax planning retroactively. You can set up a plan for 2021 all the way up till you file your taxes, which could be September or October 2022 if you file an extension. NICE!

WRITTEN PLAN REQUIREMENTS. To qualify, the plan you set up must be in writing and must be communicated to your employees. The plan's provisions must be stated in the plan. It is not sufficient for the plan to merely refer to a requirement of the Internal Revenue Code.

9. Once my eQRP is set up and I receive my plan documents how do I invest?

Your bank account is set up as part of the account setup. If you also want a brokerage account that will be included for your eQRP. Once you have this set up, you're free to invest in any allowable item by writing a check for it.

10. Do I need multiple bank accounts?

Yes, at a minimum you'll need an account for each employee's deferrals and a separate one for profit sharing. The profit-sharing account can hold all the profit sharing for all employees. If any of the employees wishes to have part or all of their contribution classified as a ROTH contribution those monies need a separate account set up.

PAYMENTS

11. Can I Rollover my existing 401k or IRA into an eQRP?

Yes, you can roll most IRA, SEP IRA, SIMPLE IRA (after 2 years), ROTH IRA (only into a Roth eQRP, 457(b), 403(b), Profit Sharing and other eQRP's into your eQRP.

In some instances, you may be able to roll funds from a 401k at a current employer through what's called an "In-Service

Distribution," although most large employers are highly restrictive and make this nearly impossible.

13. How do I calculate the amount I can contribute to my eQRP 401k and profit-sharing plan?

You can contribute up to $20,500 per year to your 401k for 2022. The profit-sharing plan will allow you to contribute a maximum of $61,000 per year for 2022 which includes the elective deferral amount ($20,500). The profit-sharing portion, which is another way of describing the employer contribution can be up to $40,500 in 2022. This amount is a maximum of 20% of the wages received by the employee if the business is a sole proprietorship, partnership or LLC.

If the business is a corporation the maximum employer contribution is 25% of the wages. So, if an employee had $90,000 in wages and the company is an LLC, he would be able to receive a maximum of $18,000 in profit sharing. If the company is a corporation, he would be able to receive up to $23,000 in profit sharing. This is in addition to the $20,500 maximum he can contribute from his wages. See the Squirrel, Rabbit and Honey Badger chapters for additional examples and information.

14. Can I buy Gold and Silver with my eQRP money? Can I keep the metals with me?

Yes, as long as you purchase the allowable bullion items (see the list in the Precious Metals section) you're allowed to purchase any of these you'd like. Since you're able to choose who will serve as trustee and if you choose yourself it's up to you to safeguard and hold assets as needed. In the case of precious metals, you (as Trustee) are able to hold them yourself in a secure facility. The IRS requires you to be a good fiduciary of the assets, meaning you must safeguard them and protect them so it would make sense to have a secure vault or safe (which could be at your home) or a safety deposit box used to store the metals.

You must also receive regular statements of value from the broker you purchase the items from. This establishes value for reporting purposes on form 5500, the annual reporting form required by the IRS. At My Gold Advisor (mygoldadvisor.com), this reporting is provided at no charge to clients.

15. Can I use personal money to transfer into my plan? What money qualifies to put into the plan?

No, you cannot transfer personal money to contribute into the plan. Qualifying contributions consist of rollovers, elective deferrals, employer match contributions, employer profit sharing contributions, and qualified non-elective contributions. New deductible contributions to your plan need to be from your business account, not your personal account. They must come from wage deductions.

16. How much money can I put into the plan each year tax deferred?

2022 maximum contribution limit is $61,000. Elective Deferral limit is $20,500 in 2022 (unless you're age 50 or greater in which case you can contribute $27,000. . . that is $20,500 + the $6500 catch up contribution). Regardless of age, the Employer can provide profit sharing of up to $40,500 per person per year.

17. Can my significant other and I both participate in one plan?

Yes, you can both be listed as Trustees of the plan. As long as you both perform services for the company, you can make elective deferral and profit-sharing contributions. In 2022, you can contribute up to $61,000 each ($122,000 if married). If you are age 50 or older, you can contribute $67,500 each.

18. **Can I design my plan to allow my children to make contributions from their wages as employees of my company to my eQRP?**

Yes, when your children are old enough to do work for your business for compensation, you can pay them by using pre-tax dollars and allowing them to contribute their wages to an eQRP. If they elect, they can take their wages and contribute to Roth 401k or a traditional 401k. A child does not pay taxes on income up to 20,500. And if you pay your kids correctly they can earn the income and pay zero payroll taxes! Check with your CPA on requirements.

19. **Can my children withdraw funds from a qualified play for their college education?**

YES, but it could be subject to a 10% early withdrawal penalty if it's your plan.

If your kids have their own Roth eQRP they can use the funds for higher education with zero taxes or penalties all 100% of the money including gains.

* Plus this asset doesn't count against you or your kids for FAFSA financial aid! Epic!

MAINTENANCE

20. **What's are the ongoing responsibilities and costs involved in eQRP Administration?**

Once you're set up you'll generally have little or no ongoing expenses.

You are required to file a form 5500 with the IRS if you plan has over $250,000 in assets. If you have less then $250,000 and less then 100 employees you're exempt from filing this form. You can file the form yourself online or you can have an advisor file the form.

The eQRP Company prepares this form for clients.

Any asset like real estate or precious metals requires a statement of value or appraisal at least once a year to be used for compliance with plan asset value reporting. Precious metals firms generally do not do this. My Gold Advisor LLC provides this as a complimentary service to clients. Non-clients may request this appraisal for a nominal fee.

A plan must have at least one fiduciary (a person or entity) named in the written plan, or through a process described in the plan, as having control over the plan's operation. The named fiduciary can be identified by office or by name. For some plans, it may be an administrative committee or a company's board of directors.

The duty to act prudently is one of a fiduciary's central responsibilities under ERISA. It requires expertise in a variety of areas, such as investments. Lacking that expertise, a fiduciary will want to hire someone with that professional knowledge to carry out the investment and other functions. Prudence focuses on the process for making fiduciary decisions. Therefore, it is wise to document decisions and the basis for those decisions. For instance, in hiring any plan service provider, a fiduciary may want to survey a number of potential providers, asking for the same information and providing the same requirements. By doing so, a fiduciary can document the process and make a meaningful comparison and selection.

21. Do I have to contribute to my eQRP every year?

NO, you can contribute whenever you want with your elective deferral (your own contribution). You have a maximum that you can contribute, but no minimum requirement.

22. The actual plan doesn't have fees, but where could fees pop up?

Fees are just one of several factors fiduciaries need to consider in deciding on service providers and plan investments. When the fees for services are paid out of plan assets, fiduciaries will want to understand the fees and expenses charged and the services provided. While the law does not specify a permissible level of fees, it does require that fees charged to a plan be "reasonable." After careful evaluation during the initial selection, the plan's fees and expenses should be monitored to determine whether they continue to be reasonable.

In comparing estimates from prospective service providers, ask which services are covered for the estimated fees and which are not. Some providers offer a number of services for one fee, sometimes referred to as a "bundled" services arrangement. Others charge separately for individual services. Compare all services to be provided with the total cost for each provider. Consider whether the estimate includes services you did not specify or want. Remember, all services have costs.

Some service providers may receive additional fees from investment vehicles, such as mutual funds, that may be offered under an employer's plan. For example, mutual funds often charge fees to pay brokers and other salespersons for promoting the fund and providing other services. There also may be sales and other related charges for investments offered by a service provider. The information provided by service providers noted above should include a description of all compensation related to the services to be provided that the service providers expect to receive directly from the plan as well as the compensation they expect to receive from other sources.

Who pays the fees? Plan expenses may be paid by the employer, the plan, or both. In addition, for expenses paid by the plan, they may be allocated to participants' accounts in a variety of ways.

23. **How much more money can I save for emergencies or retirement if I take advantage of an eQRP, instead of putting it into a savings account? (before taxes vs. after taxes)**

Scenario #1 and 2 show examples of investing money with an eQRP by taking advantage of tax deferral opportunities inside the plan. Some IRA's also allow you to invest with pre-tax dollars. HOWEVER, they do not allow for the HUGE tax saving opportunities, investment opportunities, flexibility, hardship withdrawals, and many other key elements that are allowed in an eQRP.

MORE SPECIFICS

24. **Who can be a trustee on the plan?**

You or any other person you appoint to be a trustee.

25. **Can an outside financial or legal entity (i.e., bank, law firm, CPA, trustee company, etc.) serve as trustee for a 401k?**

Technically the answer is "yes," but it is not typical or financially appropriate in today's small plan marketplace, because outside trustees add additional costs to the operation of pension plans and may or may not add any benefit. Even with an outside trustee it is impossible for the employer to transfer any legal liability away from himself. The outside trustee will not reduce the employer's liabilities or responsibilities to the plan by one atom! In the past decade virtually all new small pension plans have been set-up to be self-trustee precisely because it is less expensive, and there is no benefit doing it differently.

Outside trustees typically charge 1/2 % to 1% of the plan assets per year for their services, which amount to inspecting investment statements and certifying their accuracy. With our eQRP plans, monthly statements are sent to the plan participants and employer directly from the custodian investment companies; It is both inefficient and wasteful to pay an outside trustee to certify statements that originate from an SEC-regulated custodian such as a mutual fund investment company. 401k Pro plans are IRS-approved to be employer-trusteed. (The IRS has allowed retirement plans to be employer-trusteed since 1962).

26. Is the eQRP set up with me being the administrator, or can someone else be the administrator? What are the duties of an administrator?

You can be the administrator or hire a 3rd party to be the administrator.

Duties include:

❑ Make contributions in accordance with the plan.
❑ Keep the plan up to date and in compliance with all retirement plan laws.
❑ Invest plan assets in accordance with the plan.
❑ Provide information and required disclosures to plan participants.
❑ Distribute benefits in accordance with the plan.
❑ Inform eligible employees about the plan.

27. Under law how long must plan administer or plan provider keep 401k-related records?

The requirement is that records must be retained for 6 years. Records used to compile information that is required to be reported under the reporting and disclosure rules must be preserved by plan administrators (and by actuaries, accountants and others who may be involved) for 6 years after the due date for filing the documents to which they relate (ERISA Sec. 107). These records must have sufficient detail to permit the necessary basic information and data to be verified, explained or clarified for accuracy and are to include vouchers, worksheets, receipts, and applicable resolutions.

Accidental destruction of records will not discharge the persons required to retain records from their statutory duty with regard to the purposes for which such records are required to be retained. Where persons required to retain records know or should know that such reconstruction is impossible, or possible only at an excessive or unreasonable cost, such persons would not be under a duty to reconstruct or attempt to reconstruct the lost or destroyed records.

28. What investments can my eQRP purchase?

- ❑ Gold Bullion coins and bars must be .9999 fine
- ❑ Silver Bullion coins and bars must be .999 fine
- ❑ U.S. Treasury Gold and Silver Coins
- ❑ Small business start ups
- ❑ Tax Lien Certificates
- ❑ Trust Deeds
- ❑ Mortgage Notes
- ❑ Single Family and Multi Unit Homes
- ❑ Securities
- ❑ CD's
- ❑ Stocks
- ❑ Bonds

- ❑ Mutual Funds
- ❑ LLC's
- ❑ Apartment Buildings
- ❑ Co-Ops
- ❑ Condominiums
- ❑ Commercial Property
- ❑ Joint Ventures
- ❑ Improved or Unimproved Land
- ❑ Commodities
- ❑ Futures
- ❑ Contracts of Sale
- ❑ Factoring
- ❑ Like and Unlike Exchanges
- ❑ Leases
- ❑ Palladium.

29. Can I buy life insurance with this plan?

Yes, you can buy life insurance with an eQRP. This can dramatically cut life insurance costs by allowing premiums to be paid with mostly tax deductible rather than after tax dollars. The Tax Code also allows you to deduct the plan contributions that are used to pay for life insurance premiums. Life Insurance is not allowed in an IRA.

30. What investments are disallowed by the plan?

Anything considered a collectible, such as:

- ❑ Art
- ❑ Rugs
- ❑ Stamps or Collectible Coins
- ❑ Metal or Gem
- ❑ Antiques

31. Who can I invest with, are there any restrictions?

Anyone except disqualified persons. There is a list of disqualified people in question 86.

ROLLOVERS

32. What type of retirement accounts can I rollover into my new eQRP?

You can roll most IRA, SEP IRA, SIMPLE IRA (after 2 years), and other plans into your eQRP.

Almost any traditional IRA can be rolled into an eQRP.

In some instances, you may be able to roll funds from a 401k at a current employer through what's called an "In-Service Distribution," although most large employers are highly restrictive and make this nearly impossible.

33. If I have an existing 401k or IRA from an old employer, can I roll that into the new plan?

Yes. There are no taxes to pay or penalties if it is an in-kind roll over.

34. What if I retire early from my job, can I take my 401k or Profit Sharing out early and roll it over into the eQRP?

Yes. This is a perfect example of where the rollover allowances are so helpful. You can roll over any retirement account into an equal account.

35. I own stocks and bonds and an IRA and want to rollover these assets to the eQRP. Do I need to sell the stocks or can I roll them over to the eQRP? Do you have to sell the asset first?

You do not need to sell the stocks. You can simply roll them into the eQRP. This is called an In-Kind rollover.

WHAT YOU CAN DO WITH THE MONEY IN A eQRP

36. Do I get complete checkbook control of the plan assets?

Yes, since you are able to serve as the administrator you select who will sign the checks for the accounts the plan holds. You would normally be the check signer. This is one of my favorite parts and probably the most significant benefit of the eQRP, it doesn't require you to hire a bank or trust company to be your trustee. You, the participant can actually serve as trustee. This means that all the assets of the eQRP trust are under the sole authority of the participant if you're the only participant. (If you have employees you'll still have control over your assets and the profit sharing assets with checkbook control!)

An eQRP allows you to eliminate the expense and delays associated with an IRA custodian, enabling you to act quickly when the you find an investment you'd like to move on.

37. Can my eQRP purchase real estate I already own?

No, you must purchase real estate initially with the plan. You can purchase new real estate with your retirement plan, but if you already own the property, there is nothing to purchase, you own it.

38. How can I invest in real estate with an eQRP?

The same way you'd invest in any real estate. Once you have the eQRP set up you'll have total control of your funds so anything you want to invest in you simply write a check. If you want to invest in something requiring debt you can do that as long as you're not guaranteeing it and its non-recourse. IRA's can't do this.
Are there any restrictions on what type of property you can invest in?

There are no restrictions. You can invest in any type of property you would like, as long as you don't already own it.

39. Can I use debt in my investments from my plan?

Yes, qualified debt is permitted. Qualified debt is any debt that is nonrecourse used to purchase assets for the plan.

40. Can I personally borrow money from the plan? What are the terms of this loan?

Yes. You can borrow up to $50,000 or ½ of the vested balance, whichever is less. The loan must be amortized over a period of no more than 5 years (except for loans used to purchase a personal residence). The loan must charge a reasonable interest rate and monthly payments in substantially equal amounts must be made.

41. Can you co-mingle personal assets and bank loans with eQRP funds?

NO, never co-mingle personal assets & eQRP funds. This will get you into deep water with the IRS and could have your plan disqualified. If you have an investment you'd like to invest with personal funds and eQRP funds you can probably do that as long as each piece is separate.

42. Can I loan family or friends money out of the plan as an investment?

You can loan money to anyone except a disqualified person (see list of disqualified parties), but the loan has to have adequate security. You, as the trustee, must make sure the security is adequate in case of loan default.

43. How do you allow the employees to buy mutual funds and indexes while still allowing for purchase of non-traditional investments?

You simply set up a brokerage account for the employees that they can buy mutual funds with and you can buy and hold precious metals or real estate if you want. If someone wants to buy precious metals or real estate with their money, they can do that too. It's very flexible.

- ❏ Admin's self-directed portion of the funds are held in a checking account of his choosing. The admin then has checkbook control of assets as the signer on the account. This provides immediate access to assets and zero fees or delays for investing purposes.
- ❏ Hard assets such as precious metals are allowed to be held by the Administrator/Trustee in a secure manner. The Administrator has a fiduciary responsibility to protect the assets so as long as assets are reasonably protected, he can keep them wherever he wants. This is totally disallowed by all IRA's and many self-directed 401k's

44. Can I allow my employees to invest in my company (the employer)?

Yes, you can. Plans that invest in employer stock need to consider specific rules relating to this investment. Traditional defined benefit pension plans have limits on the amount of stock and debt obligations that a plan can hold and the amount of the plan's assets that can be invested in employer securities. For 401k plans, profit sharing plans, and employee stock ownership plans, there is no limit on how much in employer securities the plans can hold if the plan documents so provide.

If an employer decides to make employer stock an investment option under the plan, proper monitoring will include ensuring that those responsible for making investment decisions, whether an investment manager or participants, have critical information about the company's financial condition so that they can make informed decisions about the stock. Participants in individual account plans must be provided an opportunity to divest their investment in publicly traded employer securities and reinvest those amounts in other diversified investment options under the plan. For employee contributions invested in employer securities, participants have the right to divest immediately. Where employer contributions are invested in employer securities, participants can divest if they have 3 years of service. This does not apply to stand-alone employee stock ownership plans where there are no employee or employer matching contributions.

A plan can buy or sell employer securities from a party in interest, such as an employer, an employee, or other related entity as described above (which would otherwise be prohibited) if it is for fair market value and no sales commission is charged. If the plan is a defined benefit plan (a traditional pension plan), the plan generally is not permitted to hold more than 10 percent of its assets in employer stock.

45. Can I invest outside of my country with this plan? Do I have to be a U.S. resident to have an eQRP?

Yes, you can make foreign investments. No, you do not have to be a U.S. citizen to have an eQRP. However, you will need a US business and address

8888888

46. Does the eQRP provide asset protection?

Yes, under ERISA (Employee Retirement Income Security Act) laws of 1974, the plan is protected from bankruptcy, creditors, and the IRS.

47. When do I pay taxes on my plan distributions to me personally?

The distributions are treated as income and are claimed on the tax return for that year. If the distributions are received in 2021, they are claimed to the IRS along with all other income for 2021 (e.g., April 15th, 2022), and all applicable taxes will be paid at that time.

A 20% withholding is often required for distributions unless the plan is a ROTH plan. A ROTH plan is not subject to withholding when a distribution is made because the distribution is 100% tax free assuming the account holder is at least 59 1/2. A rollover is not subject to taxation.

48. Do I have to file anything with the IRS when I finally start taking distributions? What is my accountant going to need for this plan?

You will need to file Form 1099R which reports income to the IRS. The eQRP Company provides all 1099R's for clients at no charge. You also have to file a form 945V with the tax withholdings. This is due Jan 31 the year after the distribution

Your accountant will need Form 5500 annually to report assets, contributions, and number of employees. A one-person plan is exempt from filing Form 5500 is the plan assets are less than $250,000. The eQRP Company provides all required 5500 forms for clients at no charge.

49. Who does the bookkeeping for my plan?

The Plan Administrator is responsible for the bookkeeping. This can be done using QuickBooks or other accounting programs for most small plans. Hiring a TPA, Third Party Administrator to serve this purpose is useful as the complexity of the plan increases. Employers often hire outside professionals (sometimes called third-party service providers) or, if applicable, use an internal administrative committee or human resources department to manage some or all of a plan's day-to-day operations. Indeed, there may be one or a number of officials with discretion over the plan. These are the plan's fiduciaries.

50. Does every participant in my plan need to have a separate bank account?

In a 401k plan, every participant will have a separate account. This helps to keep accurate records of elective deferrals.

In a ROTH 401k plan, every participant will need a separate account.

In a Profit Sharing/Matching plan, there is one account for all employees. Contributions are accounted for on a vesting schedule which is handled by the Trustee.

51. I would like to pay for the startup costs for the plan out of an existing IRA. Is this a good idea?

Yes, this is a great idea because the plan is using pre-tax money to pay for the expense.

If your business pays for the set up costs it will get a tax deduction for the cost of the plan and may even qualify for the Small Business Tax Credit.

52. How long does it take to get the plan up and running?

Once you submit your information, you'll generally receive your plan documents from the firm in 1-2 days or less. Once you receive the documents, your bank account will be opened and you'll be able to begin making contributions and rolling funds over.

53. How does the process work after I pay to have a plan set up?

The process is simple.

- ❏ eQRP company will prepare your plan documents and upload them into your Portal.
- ❏ You will receive a digital copy of your docs after you have eSigned.
- ❏ Once the account is open, you begin making contributions from your business into your eQRP or rollover funds from your IRA, 401k, or profit-sharing plan.
- ❏ You as the Trustee can begin making investments.

54. I know that congress is trying to encourage taxpayers to set up retirement plans and has passed laws to allow tax credits for startup expenses up to $500 per year for 3 years. Is this true? And how much can I write off?

Yes. The small business startup credit is 50% of eligible start up and administrative costs, for a maximum credit of $500 per year or $1500 over 3 years, plus you can write off the balance of the cost of the plan as a business deduction. For example:

Plan cost	$4895
Year 1 tax credit:	$500
Year 1 tax deduction:	$4395
@ 40% tax bracket	<$1758> savings

Out of pocket first year: $4895 - $500 - $1758 = $2637

* In years 2 and 3 you can receive a tax credit up to $500 each year for administrative costs. So, if you have expenses for filing the 5500 form and plan filings and it cost $895, you would be able to get a tax credit of $500 from this alone.

* Savers Tax Credit: You are entitled to a tax credit of up to 50% of your contribution to a retirement plan. This provision was made a permanent part of this tax code as part of the Pension Protection Act of 2006. AGI must be less than 33,000 in 2009 for MFJ to get the full 50% Remember: a tax credit is a dollar for dollar reduction in your tax bill as opposed to a tax deduction. Married couples: get a $2,000 credit for each spouse or $4,000 total credit each year against any income taxes they owe. Saver's credit is available for IRA, eQRP, 401k, 403b, and 457 plans.

55. Is there a website I can go to for questions? Can I call you for advice on my plan and hire you later for accounting in my business?

Go to www.TheQRP.org for more detailed information regarding qualified retirement plans. Yes, feel free to call us for advice and hire us to handle the accounting for your business.

56. Do I have to file anything with the IRS?

YES, after your eQRP is setup you will need to file Form 5500 once a year if your plan assets are over $250,000, otherwise you are exempt from mandatory filing.

57. Does the eQRP have it's own Fed ID# and Separate bank account?

Yes, the Federal EIN is provided to you when the eQRP is set up, the bank account is set up at the bank or brokerage of your choosing. When you receive your eQRP book you'll receive a bank direction letter. If you have any troubles with a banker, you can always call us to to help.

58. What happens if I want to operate my business as a sole proprietorship now and then form an LLC or corporation later? Can I still use my old plan in the new LLC or Corp?

YES, that's an option. There is a 2 page adoption agreement that can be prepared for you. Your new LLC or corp can start making tax deductible contributions to the old plan just like you did before. This is generally only a few hundred dollars and gets you an entirely new and refreshed plan.

59. If I am not a U.S. resident (Canadian) can I set up a retirement plan in the U.S. and still keep my plan in a foreign county like Canada?

YES. There are no laws that prevent you from having a retirement plan in both countries.

60. When do I pay taxes on deferred income that I've contributed to my eQRP?

You'll pay taxes at your current income tax rate, which is determined by all income, including distribution income in the year that it's taken. Any portion of elective contributions identified to be ROTH (after tax contributions) will normally not have any tax owed, if distributions are done after age 59 1/2.

61. How do I set up my new eQRP bank account?

Take federal ID # and your eQRP plan documents to the bank or financial institution and open up your bank account; checking, saving, money market etc

62. I own stocks and bonds and a IRA and want to rollover to eQRP; do I need to sell the stocks or can I roll them over into the eQRP?

You do not have to sell....you simply call the current custodian of the assets and inquire into their procedure for doing a rollover into your new plan, your eQRP

63. For the 2022 year if my company is a *Sole Proprietorship, LLC or Corporation* how much time do I have to make contributions to my plan and take a tax deduction?

If you are a sole proprietor or LLC you have until you file your tax return in 2022, including any extentions for both elective deferrals and profit sharing. If you are a corporation or LLC filing as an S you must make your elective deferral contributions through wages paid by Dec 31, 2021 and profit sharing can be contributed from the company though the date of filing the corporate return including extensions.

64. I have a Corporation and pay myself a $30,000 annual salary.What is the maximum amount I can contribute to my plan?

If you are over age 50 you could contribute $27,000 plus profit sharing of up to 25% of the wages above the $27,000, so another $1000 for profit sharing. If you're younger than 50 your contribution would be approximately $23,000 maximum.

65. Do you need profits in order to make contributions to a Profit-Sharing Plan?

NO. Of course having profit would probably make it easier to actually contribute something however, contribution to a profit sharing plan is discretionary. There is no set amount of profits that you need to make to contribute to profit-sharing plans.

66. What's the difference between Elective and Non-Elective Contributions?

Elective contributions are optional contributions made by an employee, non-elective contributions are not options and are required to be made by certain employees in the case of a Safe Harbor plan.

67. What disclosures are needed for the Safe Harbor plan or with employees?

What the employer is going to contribute and how they will contribute each year to the safe harbor plan must be disclosed to the participants prior to the beginning of each plan year. In 2011 the DOL issued final rules mandating the disclosure of specific investment and fee information to participants in self-directed account plans subject to ERISA. These final rules require that certain disclosures, including detailed plan-related information and investment-related information, be included in an initial notice, which will also be updated and re-issued on an annual basis.

http://www.mwe.com/DOL-Issues-Electronic-Guidelines-for-New-2012-Participant-Investment-and-Fee-Disclosures-02-15-2012/

These plan related items include the fees associated with the administration of the plan, outside of the investment itself, and what method of allocation the employer chooses. The disclosure forms must also tell the employees who the designated investment managers are. There are limits to what the employee can choose to invest in, and the employer gets to choose what those limitations are, and must disclose those limitations to the employee. Among the set of limited investments, the employer is obligated to disclose performance data of those investments. Basically, the employer has to give the employee everything they need to decide which investments they want to participate in, including financial definitions.

http://www.mwe.com/publications/uniEntity.aspx?xpST=Publicat
ionDetail&pub=5517

68. How much am I required to contribute to employees with my Safe Harbor Plan?

Employers are required to contribute 3% of the employee's compensation. Once the employee is qualified, they are 100% vested.

69. Do all employees qualify for the 3% matching in my Safe Harbor plan?

No, only employees that are full time OR work at least 500 hours per year. (you can make it easier to qualify but this is the highest bar that can be set, for example you can make a 1 hour requirement or any part time employee qualifies).

They must also work at least 1 year before they are eligible for the non-elective deferral. An employer can lower this standard if desired to allow for more enrollments of employees more quickly.

70. When does an eligible employee in a Safe Harbor plan start to receive the non-elective deferral contribution?

Enrollment happens twice a year, Jan. 1 and July 1. If an employee qualifies with the amount of time working and the full time of at least 500 hours a year prior to the enrollment date they would start receiving the non-elective deferral contributions at that time.

71. What is the difference between a 401k and a Profit Sharing Plan?

The 401k generally describes the employee contribution whereas the Profit Sharing Plan is the Employer contribution.

72. Can an employer have multiple 401k plans?

Yes, but the limits for a plan are still in place for combined plans. An employer can't set up additional plans to multiply the amount being deferred. Multiple companies that are controlled or owned with a majority share by one person are considered to have a brother-sister relationship and are combined to determine contribution limit thresholds.

73. Who controls the profit sharing money and how it's invested?

The trustee controls this money and how it's invested.

74. What is a 990T?

It's the form to report Unrelated Business Income Tax. If your eQRP had active income that was taxed you would likely use this form.

75. What is the Vesting Period?

The period of time for profit sharing funds to become the property of the employee. In a Safe Harbor plan the profit sharing funds are vested immediately. In other plans the vesting can take place over a period of time up to 6 years from employee start date or all at once after a maximum of 3 years. A common approach is the graded approach where the funds are vested over time at 20% a year until the full amount contributed is the property of the employee 5 years from the date the funds are contributed. The term for a sudden full vesting is called a cliff.

76. What does it mean to be "vested" in my retirement account?

To be vested in a retirement account, simply means you can take the money with you if you leave the company. For example, if you are 75% vested, then you can take 75% of your investment with you when you leave. In a 401k plan, you are 100% vested in the money you defer into your retirement plan.

77. What are the advantages of a Qualified Plan versus an IRA?

There are many advantages of having a Qualified Retirement Plan versus and IRA. 10X the contributions, greater liability protection, ability to totally control the assets, can take custody of assets, can borrow against the plan…the list is long

78. What types of businesses can set up Qualified Retirement Plans?

Sole Proprietorship, C Corporation, S Corporation, Partnership, Limited Liability Corporation (LLC), Limited Liability Partnership (LLP), and Not for Profit 501(c)(3).

SELF DIRECTED 401k King = The eQRP

79. What is a best self-directed 401k?

A self-directed 401k is technically no different than any other 401k. It's unique because of the available investment options. Most custodians only allow approved stocks, bonds, mutual funds and CDs. A truly self-directed 401k allows those types of investments PLUS specific gold and silver, real estate, notes, private placements, tax lien certificates and much more.

80. What are the benefits of the eQRP?

In addition to the tremendous 401k benefits already discussed (tax-free profits, tax deductions, asset protection and estate planning), you can invest tax-free in investments that you know and understand, which through the power of compounding interest, can create additional wealth for you and your family.

81. Are there any negatives of the eQRP?

The eQRP does require more administration than something like an IRA. Since you, the business owner, will typically be the trustee in an eQRP, you have a fiduciary responsibility to protect assets. This responsibility is not normally required in an IRA that has a third party custodian.

82. Why haven't I heard of the eQRP before?

While the concept of investing in real estate and other assets in retirement plans has been around for more than 30 years, it hasn't received a great deal of attention. Why? Most custodians that offer 401ks (banks and brokerage firms) focus on mutual funds and CDs- because they have financial interests in having you select those investments from them. Meaning, they make money by directing and managing the investments for you. The idea here is to be in control of your own financial success.

Because a majority of custodians focus on stocks and CDs, there's a common misconception that these are your only investment options for retirement plans. But this is not the case.

83. Is the eQRP allowed under IRS rules?

Yes, as long as you follow relevant rules. IRS Publication 560 and 590 clearly state the rules and regulations governing IRAs and qualified retirement plans. You can find these publications on www.eQRP.co/560 and www.eqrp.co/590 respectively.

84. Are there special rules for the eQRP investments?

Yes. To ensure compliance, you should be familiar with specific rules for 401k's and in particular, self-directed 401ks. There are certain types of transactions that you cannot perform through a 401k. Most importantly, the IRS prohibits "self-dealing" investments in which you or family members of lineal descent have prior ownership.

85. How can I be sure that my investment is allowable in an eQRP?

IRS Publications state what investments are prohibited in all Qualified Retirement Plans. These investments include: artwork, stamps, rugs, antiques and gems.

All other investments, including stocks, bonds, mutual funds, real estate, promissory notes, foreclosures, and tax liens are acceptable as long as IRS rules governing retirement plans are followed.

86. My CPA/attorney/financial advisor hasn't heard of the eQRP? What Should I Do?

It's not uncommon for advisors to never have heard of self-directed qualified retirement plans. We have worked with many professional advisors across the country to educate them regarding eQRP's and self directed eQRP rules so they can give good financial advice to their clients.

87. Are my self directed eQRP investments guaranteed?

No investment (aside for FDIC-insured deposits) is guaranteed. However, most successful investors feel that the risk of investing in assets they know and understand is much less than the risk associated with making only conventional investments.

88. Are self directed eQRP's for everyone?

Self directed eQRPs are not for everyone. They are generally better for those who want to create wealth by using their knowledge of investing in assets other than stocks, bonds and CDs.

89. Why Should I Open eQRP plan?

The eQRP is attractive to employers and employees because of the high contribution limits and large tax deductions available. Plus, you have the ability to truly self-direct investments in traditional and non-traditional assets. Two components comprise the maximum The eQRP plan contribution:

- ❑ An employee salary-deferral contribution: In 2022, the employee can contribute up to $20,500 annually through salary deferral, although this may not exceed 100% of the employee's pay.
- ❑ An employer profit-sharing contribution: The annual limit for this is 25% of the employee's pay.

The total annual contribution limit is $61,000 in 2022. However, under a "catch up" provision, individuals age 50 and over may contribute $6500 in 2022 allowing a total contribution limit of $67,500.

90. Am I eligible for the eQRP?

The main requirement for any 401k is earned income as an employee. Employees can contribute funds on a post-tax elective deferral basis or as pre-tax deferrals under their traditional 401k plans.

Distribution from 401k Plans cannot be made until one of the following occurs.

❑ The employee retires, dies, is disabled. Or otherwise severs employment.
❑ The plan ends and no other defined contribution plan is established or continued.
❑ In the case of a 401k plan that is part of a Profit-Sharing Plan, the employee reaches age 59 ½ or suffers financial hardship.

91. What are the Prohibited transactions?

Prohibited transactions are listed in Code Section 4975 are transactions between the plan and a disqualified person that are prohibited by law. *However, see Exemption later.* If you are a disqualified person who takes part in a prohibited transaction, you must pay a tax. Prohibited transactions generally include the following transactions:

❑ A transfer of plan income or assets to, or use of them by or for the benefit of, a disqualified person.
❑ Any act of a fiduciary by which he or she deals with plan income or assets in his or her own interest.
❑ The receipt of consideration by a fiduciary for his or her own account from any party dealing with the plan in a transaction that involves plan income or assets.
❑ Examples of some common Prohibited Transactions:
❑ Selling an interest in real estate owned by the eQRP to a "Disqualified Person"
❑ Buying an interest in real estate for your eQRP from a "Disqualified Person"
❑ Selling or transferring real estate you own personally to your eQRP

- ❏ Purchasing real estate with eQRP funds and leasing to a disqualified person
- ❏ Investing eQRP funds in a house that is used by the eQRP owner or other "Disqualified Person"
- ❏ Personally guaranteeing a loan to your eQRP
- ❏ Buying real estate with your eQRP and making repairs personally or having a "Disqualified Person" make them
- ❏ Buying real estate with personal funds and then transferring title to the eQRP
- ❏ Using personal funds to pay taxes and expenses related to the eQRP plan real estate investment
- ❏ Being compensated for any services performed for or on behalf of the eQRP
- ❏ Contributing personal funds to your eQRP bank account
- ❏ Acquiring a credit card for your eQRP bank account
- ❏ Using your retirement funds to make a real estate investment and earning a commission personally from the purchase.
- ❏ Making an investments using your eQRP into a company or fund that will benefit the eQRP participant or a "Disqualified Person" personally
- ❏ Making an investment using eQRP funds to facilitate or protect the eQRP owners's investment

Any of the following acts between the plan and a disqualified person

- ❏ Selling, exchanging, or leasing property between a plan and a disqualified person
- ❏ Lending money or extending credit between a plan and a disqualified person
- ❏ Furnishing goods, services, or facilities between a plan and a disqualified person
- ❏ Transfer to or use by or for the benefit of a disqualified person of the income or assets of a plan

❑ Act by a disqualified person who is a fiduciary whereby he deals with the income or assets of a plan in his own interests or for his own account; or

❑ Receipt of any consideration for his own personal account by any disqualified person who is a fiduciary from any party dealing with a lan in connection with a transaction involving the income or assets of the plan.

EXEMPTION: Certain transactions are exempt from being treated as prohibited transactions. For example: a prohibited transaction does not take place if you are a disqualified person and receive any benefit to which you are entitled as a plan participant or beneficiary.

92. Who is a Disqualified Persons?

A Disqualified Person according to Internal Revenue Code Section 4975(e)(2) generally includes the eQRP participant, any ancestors or lineal descendants (kids or their offspring) of the plan participant, and entities in which the plan participant holds a controlling equity or management interest. Under this section a "disqualified person" means:

❑ A fiduciary (the eQRP plan participant, or person having authority over making plan investments.

❑ A person providing services to the plan (ex. the trustee or custodian)

❑ An employer, any of whole employees are covered by the eQRP

❑ An employee organization any of whose members are covered by the eQRP

❑ A 50 percent owner of C or D

❑ A family member of A, B, C or D above the lineal descendants (the participant or fiduciary's spouse, parents, grandparents, children, grandchildren, spouses of the fiduciary's children and grandchildren, but not parents in law or siblings)

❑ An entity (corporation, partnership, trust or estate) owned or controlled more then 50% by A, B, C, D, or E. Whether an entity is a disqualified person is determined by considering the indirect stockholdings/interest which would be taken into account under Code Sec. 267(c), except that members of a fiduciary's family are the family members under Code Sec. 4975(3)(6) (lineal descendants) for purpose of determining disqualified persons.

* Siblings, aunts, uncles, cousins, step siblings or friends are not treated as "Disqualified Persons"

For More information on Retirement Plans for Small Businesses please see:

http://www.irs.gov/pub/irs-pdf/p560.pdf

http://www.irs.gov/Retirement-Plans/Plan-Participant,-Employee/401k-Resource-Guide---Plan-Participants---Limitation-on-Elective-Deferrals

Made in the USA
Middletown, DE
22 February 2022

61675647R00109